SURVIVING THIS

BABYLON

ANCIENT SECRETS FOR MODERN SURVIVAL

O!
What a Savior!

DR. DOUGLAS LEVESQUE

Doug Levesque
Dan. 6:3

ISBN: 0692495061
ISBN-13: 9780692495063

DEDICATION

To Immanuel Baptist Church
of
Corunna, Michigan

You are the living model of an excellent spirit!
Congratulations on 20 years.
May you survive and thrive for 20 more.

ACKNOWLEDGMENTS

My gratitude runs deep. My wife Amy is the best Christian and person I know. Her spirit is perpetually "preferred above" all others. She overflows with all of the "secrets" shared in this book. Our sons easily call her "blessed, and so does everybody else! To her I owe many thanks as every project I do is a collaborative effort with her. Thank you, darling.

Also, I must give a hearty "Bravo!" to my co-laborers John Bronkema, Terry Brewer, Charlie Nash, John Pullen and Gil Humphreys. Your backing in all things strengthens my spine and propels my feet. Jim Demis, Ed Shumaker, Don Musser, and Phil Stewart all prop me up. You make me look MUCH better than I truly am. What a fantastic core of Daniel-like men you all are to me. Pass the baton, but keep on running!

We may be in Babylon, but we know how to beat it!

To our staff and publishing crew, thanks. Now, there is more work to do.

TABLE OF CONTENTS

Preface: It Can be Done   i

Introduction: "This Babylon"   1

Part One: An Excellent Spirit

1. Daniel's Dilemma   13

2. The Spirit of God in Man   21

3. Factor One: A Relationship with God   31

4. Factor Two: Enthusiasm for a Holy Life   41

5. Factor Three: An Attitude "From Above"   49

6. Factor Four: Priorities From Heaven   57

7. Factor Five: A Disciplined Stewardship   65

8. Daniel's Defiance R.E.A.P.S.
    Survival and More   75

Part Two: The Example of an Excellent Spirit Through the Ages

9. Daniel's Legacy   87

10. The Persian Expression of Babylon   95

11. The Greek Expression of Babylon   103

12. The Roman Expression of Babylon   111

13. The Modern Expression of Babylon   119

Conclusion: What Disparate Enemies Have in Common

129

Appendix

A. Mystery, Babylon – The Pope and President Do Business Together   137

B. Constantine the Great – Was He a Christian?   147

C. Undermining the Nation State   153

D. Secrets of the U.N. Meditation Room   159

E. Jesus, About Himself   163

PREFACE
It Can be Done

The Bible is filled with historical accounts of "evil empires" and their "despot rulers". The reality of such difficult circumstances for Bible adherents of the past is something we often look back on and thank God we do not have to endure. However, in recent years, even the United States has become more and more "Babylonian." Today, the Bible is being relegated to a myth or just a book among books. Bible believers are increasingly being hushed in the public arena. Bible speak is hardly being tolerated, even in church services. Bible literacy is at alarmingly low levels. Could it be possible for "evil empires" and "despot rulers" to once again claim a place of power and influence? How will this affect Bible believers? Is there a way to survive such "Babylonian" circumstances? Can one be an adamant Bible advocate and still thrive? We can find the answers to these questions in the Bible itself, and we can take heart at the hope that is offered.

Many are intimidated by and afraid of what may be happening to their freedoms in America today. Conspiracy theories and even paranoia abound, but the reactions to these mindsets – apathy, malaise, and surrender – are even worse. A Biblical response is in order. The proper response is to stand with an adamant purpose to survive and thrive in modern "Babylonian" societies. Consider the following Bible vignettes:

1. Joseph in Egypt

"And Pharaoh said unto Joseph, See, I have set thee over all the land of Egypt." -Genesis 41:41.

The Pharaohs were not known for their kindness, especially to the Hebrews, but in the midst of his life gone mad, Joseph not only survived, but thrived. Joseph continued to walk with and trust Almighty God. This made him a humble and able servant. God touched all that Joseph did, making Joseph appear to have the Midas touch. Everyone wanted a bit of Joseph's "magic". Joseph took none of the glory for himself, and eventually he became a savior of his family and of much of the ancient world.

2. Daniel in Babylon

"Then this Daniel was preferred above the presidents and princes, because an excellent spirit was in him; and the king thought to set him over the whole realm." -Daniel 6:3.

Nebuchadnezzar, Belshazzar, Darius, and Cyrus – these are just some of the pagan rulers with whom Daniel had to deal. His oppressors were ruthless in their conquest. Daniel held to the Bible and its truths time and again. He was hated, plotted against, and betrayed, but he maintained an "excellent spirit" throughout every ordeal. Somehow, he always stayed close to the seat of power and influenced it, over and over, for the preservation of his people. Perhaps he read the proverb,

"He that hath knowledge spareth his words: and a man of understanding is of an excellent spirit."
–Proverbs 17:27.

3. Mordecai in Persia

"For Mordecai was great in the king's house, and his fame went out throughout all the provinces: for this man Mordecai waxed greater and greater."
-Esther 9:4.

No person can deny that Persian culture was opposed to Biblical influences. King Ahasuerus reigned from India to Ethiopia with an iron hand. His lieutenant, Haman, was very averse to the Biblical culture of the Jews and schemed for their destruction. The king was an immoral man with poor judgment, but could not deny the loyal service and skillful diplomacy of Mordecai – or the beauty of Esther. Of course, Mordecai was Esther's chief influence, and he raised her in the way of the Word. When it came time to fulfill her destiny, she did not blink.

4. Paul in Rome

"All the saints salute you, chiefly they that are of Caesar's household." -Philippians 4:22.

While Nero remains one of the most infamously murderous Caesars to this day, Paul actually used his Roman citizenship for an advantage in the work of the Gospel ministry. His "appeal to Caesar" not only spared his life for years to come, but got him free passage to Rome at Rome's expense. Along the way, he won over his shipmates, housemates, and even his guards. He preached to kings and governors. Ultimately, he was able to preach the Gospel to Nero himself on at least two occasions. He was successful in converting some of Caesar's own house. Today, Paul's letter to the Romans is printed and shared in most of the languages of the world.

These men shared the ancient secrets of survival. Rightly understood and applied, these secrets will help you survive in this modern Babylon as well.[1] It can be done!

---

[1] Preface reprinted from the *Bible Nation Magazine,* March 2007.

INTRODUCTION
This Babylon

"Babylon has veered from being the <u>center</u> of mighty empires to the <u>symbol</u> of the most repressive regimes, and in the Bible is <u>synonymous</u> with everything that is sinful against God and His kingdom"[1] *[emphasis added]*

-Dr. Norman Bancroft Hunt, Fellow of the Royal Anthropological Institute

Ancient Babylon. It can only be imagined now. Its grandness and its total pervasiveness of early culture is well-represented in history. Its legendary mixing of

---

[1] Norman Bancroft Hunt, *A Historical Atlas of Ancient Mesopotamia* (New York: Checkmark Books, 2004), 122.

political power and religious control has been the foundation for every succeeding empire – Persian, Greek, and Roman. European and Oriental monarchs have since been both head of state and head of a national church in some form. While this arrangement imagines a perfect recipe for power and prosperity, no such totalitarian system has been able to usher in or serve up the platter of utopian perfection. In fact, this Babylonian architecture of society is consistently romanticized and reborn under new banners offering "new" old promises. Russian Czars, British Kings, German Fuhrers, and ISIS Mahdi's all reflect a Babylonian construct, albeit with Roman swag. Although this paradigm always ends badly, the idea never really goes away. It does not die; it re-trenches and comes back, often reformed and more attractive. This is what is meant by the Apostle John in the Revelation, "Behold, Mystery, Babylon." It is a last days, ultra-modern, technologically advanced Babylonian reboot. It smiles and offers a hope, but it is the salesmanship of a whore, "the mother of all harlots".

2

Its intention is not honest but perverse, and seduces us into a wicked "fornication" between government and religion. The final manifestation of THIS Babylon is alive and well today. This treatise will clearly identify THIS Babylon for you. It is evil and rapidly growing into a global apparition. Its goal is now what it has always been . . . politically, to rule the world, and spiritually, to defy Almighty God and enthrone the rebellious creation, Lucifer. War against Scripture, Saint, and Savior is upon you. This book is a survival manual, both physical and spiritual, instructing you in the art and science of **SURVIVING THIS BABYLON.**

In the fifth century B.C., Greek historian Herodotus describes the ancient city thusly:

> "The city stands on a broad plain, and is **an exact square**, a hundred and twenty furlongs in length each way, so that the entire circuit is four hundred and eighty furlongs. While such is its size, **in magnificence there is no other city that approaches to it.** It is surrounded, in the first place, by a broad and deep moat, full of water, behind which rises a wall fifty royal cubits in width, and two hundred in

3

height. The top, along the edges of the wall, they constructed buildings of a single chamber facing one another, leaving between them room for a **four-horse chariot** to turn. In the circuit of the wall are a hundred gates, all of brass, with brazen lintels and side-posts."[2]

Herodotus may have been exaggerating, but not by much.

Visually, Babylon was a city "foursquare" of unprecedented immensity and grandeur. It was a human reflection, or perhaps a demonic mockery, of the heavenly city described in Revelation. It was a satanically inspired, heaven-like city, secretly proposing hellish intentions. Its accommodating of four horses on the wall is an eerily prophetic foreshadowing of Revelation as well. "The city was built upon the Euphrates, and divided in equal parts along its left and right banks, with steep embankments to contain the

---

[2] George Rawlinson, *The History of Herodotus*, ed., vol. 1 (New York: D. Appleton and Company, 1885), 178-200.

river's seasonal floods."[3] In essence, a river ran through it. This vision of a ruling city was reflected in America's own capitol, Washington D.C., by its architects.[4] "Originally, D.C. was a quadrilateral of 4 borderlines that were each 10 miles long."[5] In other words, a city foursquare, with a river running through it by design. Although the Babylonish ideals, assumed in the Egyptian and Roman-Greco style, are aesthetically stunning, their literal "reflection" in the reflection pool on the National Mall has esoteric meaning. Many have called this fact out through America's centuries. Some have even stopped or destroyed the more brazen aspects of ancient meanings, but the "mystery of iniquity doth already work" and is prevailing here, in America, visually, as it has elsewhere in history. Lastly, modern

---

[3] "Babylon," *Wikipedia*, last modified July 13, 2015, accessed July 17, 2015, https://en.wikipedia.org/wiki/Babylon.

[4] The work of André Le Nôtre, particularly his Gardens of Versailles, is said to have influenced L'Enfant's master plan for the capital. https://en.wikipedia.org/wiki/L%27Enfant_Plan.

[5] *"How Big is Washington, DC?,"* accessed July 17, 2015, http://www.washingtondc-go.com/facts/how-big-is-dc.html.

digital media is both personal and prevailing. It rapidly spreads the visual imagery of THIS Babylon – think of the Olympic opening ceremonies and the American halftime shows. These are mini pagan festivals right off the streets of Babylon itself. THIS Babylon is appearing before our very eyes.

Politically, it was an empire of perhaps 127 states, ruled by a monarch who was perceived to be a god. Nebuchadnezzar, meaning "Nebo protect the crown", was a Czar, a Caesar, as the sound of his name predicts. Nebo was, according to Strong's Concordance, a "Babylonian deity who presided over learning and letters; correspond(ing) to Greek Hermes, Latin Mercury, and Egyptian Thoth." There was no separation of church and state, thus the Biblical narrative highlights this political-religious despotism in the fact that Nebuchadnezzar erected a golden monolith to be exclusively worshipped, along with orchestrated music and political enforcement. A sort of "nation state" idolatry defines THIS Babylon, ancient or modern, and is evident in Hitler's Nazi state construct, is like the Sunni Baathist ideology, and more recently, in our own nascent, western forms of allegiance (a.k.a. NATO or the U.N.). American presidential iconoclasts are, as the Constitutional mist burns off our republicanism, hardly different than their Babylonian predecessors. Statues, monuments, coinage, and even Mt. Rushmore are no longer as innocent as once posited. It was Christian influence that originally demanded separation of powers, and of the state from stopping free exercise of religion; Christians demanded the bill of rights, recognizing the potential danger of any government document. They held off until now, politically, THIS Babylon. Christian America was being usurped by a masonic representation of Babylon from day one.

Spiritually, the prophet Jeremiah saw Babylon for what it was, <u>an ethereal enemy manifest through a man and a political-religious system</u>. He warned of it. He watched it conquer and crush his home. Finally, he wept and lamented in the ashes over its desolating evil. He prophesied:

"Thus saith the LORD, . . . Flee out of the midst of Babylon, and deliver every man his soul: be not cut off in her iniquity; for this is the time of the LORD'S vengeance; he will render unto her a recompence. Babylon hath been a golden cup in the LORD'S hand, that made all the earth drunken: the nations have drunken of her wine; therefore the nations are mad."
-Jeremiah 51:1, 6-7.

The prophet Daniel interpreted Nebuchadnezzar's troubling yet foretelling political and spiritual dream of a multi-metaled man by saying , "Thou art THIS head of gold." He went on to forecast the Silver Empire of the Persians, the Bronze Age of the Greeks, the Iron Power of Rome, the divided power of the Byzantines, and a final mysterious form of a clay-iron mix. An empire of toes, partly weak and partly strong, yet altogether Babylon, is here. Babylon then, unto Babylon now, transformed into modernity, is the same oppressive evil. THIS modern Babylon poses its greatest threat, a maniacal and homicidal one to all earth's inhabitants today, yet many are transfixed by her still. In Revelation, the beast out of the sea and the beast out of the earth are two men. Similarly, the images of the beast ridden and the whore riding are two systems, Politics and Religion, conspired together to resurrect THIS Babylon. Recognizing THIS Babylon is the first step in surviving. Responding properly is the next step. In the first chapter, you will see how Daniel survived and even thrived in Babylon. Good reading!

PART ONE:
AN EXCELLENT SPIRIT

CHAPTER ONE
Daniel's Dilemma

"Daniel does not give a continued history of the reigns in which he lived, nor of the state-affairs of the kingdoms of Chaldea and Persia, though he was himself a great man in those affairs; for what are those to us? But he selects such particular passages of story as serve for the confirming of our faith in God and the encouraging of our obedience to him, <u>for the things written aforetime were written for our learning.</u> It is a very observable improvable story that we have in this chapter, how Daniel by faith "stopped the mouths of lions, and so obtained a good report," Heb. 11:33." [1]

-Matthew Henry, Welsh non-conformist minister (1708–1710)

---

[1] Matthew Henry, *An Exposition of the Old and New Testament* (London: Joseph Ogle Robinson, 1828)

Overwhelming Circumstances. That sums up Daniel's dilemma. He was, as a youth, set into slavery and cast out of his country. He watched a wicked foreign power march upon his homeland, humble his king, and make a mockery of his God. He may have been of noble birth, yet he must have felt a promising future slipping away. He knew God and His word intimately, and trusted in Him completely, yet still had to, by providence or by consequence, experience defeat and disaster. He lived under the palace eunuchs, and some scholars think he was made into one himself. We never hear of Daniel owning property, getting married, having children, or receiving liberty. He was surrounded by envious pagans, killer warriors, and ambitious royals. It must have been sheer torture at times. The trip to Babylon; hunger and thirst; blood and carnage; the unknown languages and practices of paganism would have been frightful for a young Hebrew. Will I survive? Will I suffer pain? Will I ever see my family again? Are they alive? Is Israel gone? What is God doing? Whatever overwhelming circumstances modern man is in now or about to experience, Daniel would understand. His advice would be helpful right about now. How did he survive such a tsunami of Babylonian horror? How do we now?

> *"Then this Daniel was preferred above the presidents and princes, because an excellent spirit was in him; and the king thought to set him over the whole realm."* *-Daniel 6:3.*

"Preferred above presidents and princes," is certainly a full resume on Daniel's capacity to overcome his Babylonian circumstances. In fact, Daniel survived seventy years of Babylon's evil! He did so as a glorified servant, lifted up as what amounted to a vice presidency, by what could equate to seven different kings and five different administrations. That would be like one person staying under twelve presidents from F.D.R to Barack Hussein Obama. Amazing! Wars and scandals came and went, but Daniel stayed. Liberals and Conservatives (or the Babylonian equivalents) rose and fell, but Daniel maintained. Laws passed, technologies developed,

15

media reported, generations passed, yet Daniel toughed it out. He never compromised himself or his faith. He never lived without risk of death. He did not give in to self-interest or an easier path. We do not know what level of fear he had to deal with, but his fear and reverence for the Almighty must have trumped all. Where did this "preference" come from? How did a Jew from Israel gain such standing and influence in Babylon? How can we survive the coming onslaught, and then come out "preferred" after all? It was not easy. Daniel did suffer, and greatly. But, despite the sure hardship, it was possible. The answer is staring you in the face.

"...Because an **excellent spirit** was in him;"

Through the hardships, in spite of circumstances, and in the face of devilish designs, Daniel had an excellent spirit. He was given the Babylonian name of Belteshazzar, or according to Gesenius' Lexicon, "the prince whom Bel favors". This is no endorsement of Babylon's paganism, but the recognition that even in their Luciferian cult, Daniel's "spirit," and therefore his spirituality, was uniquely recognized and trusted. All of the wise men, Chaldeans, and magicians could not divine the times or answer the ultimate questions to satisfy the kings' inquiries. They could not produce the real results or match the productive counsel of the lowly Daniel. Somehow, he was more noble than all the noblemen between the Nile and the Indus Rivers. His brand of spirituality was more potent than all the shamans from Africa, Mesopotamia, and India. A conquered slave had risen to prominence within the Babylonian system. Only the Head Potentate, the King, ranked in authority above the faithful young man who seemed to have the "favor of the gods." Daniel did not masquerade under the charade of his assumed name, but honestly spoke of His one true God. His survival was due to the Person's Spirit that resided "in him." A Person's Spirit in him that was higher and more powerful than all the masters of Babylon itself.

"...And the king thought to set him over the whole realm." A trustworthy, honest man that is productive and harmless can gain preference among his enemies and turn their venom against themselves. Daniel did not set out to conquer, only to survive. He could not compromise his God, but he could endure suffering in His name. Lesser men give in to Babylon. They even become "Babylonian" for their survival. In the end, they neither thrive nor survive, but end up mad, humiliated, burnt, or lion food. The accounts of Daniel teach us much. They are a blueprint for surviving the last day's Babylonian oppression. The global government and religious structure falling into power over us now is not unlike the "golden head" by which Daniel was conquered.[2] The clay-iron toes of Daniel's interpretation, a modern polyglot of the golden past, threatens humanity with the ugliest cages of imprisonment yet. The feet wish to stomp out the earth, but the rock comes out of nowhere to smash the Babylonian man and all his

---

[2] See Appendix C: Undermining the Nation State

elements.[3] Daniel's victory foreshadows our own.

The nineteenth century Baptist pulpiteer, Charles Haddon Spurgeon, spoke of Daniel's dilemma:

"Daniel was a man in very high position in life. It is true he was not living in his own native land, but, in the providence of God, he had been raised to great eminence under the dominion of the country in which he dwelt. He might, therefore, naturally have forgotten his poor kinsmen; many have done so. Alas! we have known some that have even forgotten their poor fellow Christians when they have grown in grace, and have thought themselves too good to worship with the poorer sort when they themselves have grown rich in this world's goods. But it was not so with Daniel. Though he had been made a president of the empire, yet he was still a Jew; he felt himself still one with the seed of Israel. In all the afflictions of his people he was afflicted, and he felt it his honour to be numbered with them, and his duty and his privilege to share with them all the bitterness of their lot. If he could not become despised and as poor as they, if God's providence had made him to be distinguished, yet **his heart would make no distinction**: he would remember them and pray for them, and would plead that their desolation might yet be removed."[4]

---

[3] Daniel 2:43-45.

[4] Charles Haddon Spurgeon, "Daniel: A Pattern for Pleaders," sermon No. 3484, published November 4, 1915.

Daniel prayed for them then and for us now:

"O Lord, hear; O Lord, forgive; O Lord, hearken and do; defer not, for thine own sake, O my God: for thy city and thy people are called by thy name."
—Daniel 9:19.

Daniel overcame his circumstances through exercising an excellent spirit. It is how he survived Babylon. It is the same way you will survive THIS Babylon. An excellent spirit is not simply a positive attitude or a happy-go-lucky demeanor, but it is the very person of God within a human soul, eternalizing it and making it, in human terms, excellent.

CHAPTER TWO
The Spirit of God in Man

"It is easier to describe such a life, and to understand how it could be lived, than it is to reproduce it. And yet the God of Daniel liveth; there is no change in him. Only we lack the faith of Daniel, and from that lack all our difficulties spring. Could we but "see him who is invisible," we might rival him whose faith "stopped the mouths of lions."[1] *-William M. Taylor*

God is a Person. He is not simply a theoretical idea, an impersonal force or an imaginary friend. He presents Himself, His names, and His attributes all together as a personality that can be known. He wants to be known.

[1] William M. Taylor, *Daniel the Beloved* (Belfast: Ambassador Production Ltd., 1878), 232.

He can be personally known, not just known about. This autobiography called Scripture is "of no private interpretation."[2] Although different people mishandle the divine invitation to "know me," and so mistakenly re-shape God into graven images, self-made ideals, or a pantheon of heroes, we will one day see Him face to face and be fully immersed in His exact and poignant beauty. In His ethereal form, the Spirit, God "moved upon the face of the waters"[3] to create the material world. This same Spirit "overshadowed" the virgin girl, Mary, and promised, the "holy thing which shall be born...shall be called the Son of God."[4] Her espoused husband, Joseph the carpenter, was told by the angel Gabriel that his name would be Jesus. The shepherds were told that he would be called "Saviour". Isaiah, a prophet, foretold that he

---

[2] 2 Peter 1:20, all Scripture references are taken from the Authorized Version, KJV.

[3] Genesis 1:2.

[4] Luke 1:35.

would be called "the mighty God."[5] God reveals that He moves and works as a timeless Spirit, therefore knows "the end from the beginning,"[6] and that in Him there "is no variableness, neither shadow of turning."[7] Therefore, being limitless and all powerful, He yet humbled Himself for our benefit and was "made flesh"[8] as a man. Jesus grew as a man, suffered as a man, died as a man, and was buried as a man. He never sinned. But He rose, showing Himself different, the only "God-man." "God is a spirit,"[9] He taught. "Ye believe in God, believe also in me,"[10] He affirmed. "He that hath seen me hath seen the Father,"[11] He proclaimed. Jesus claimed to be the very incarnate person of God. He was visible, audible,

---

[5] Isaiah 9:6.

[6] Isaiah 46:10.

[7] James 1:17.

[8] John 1:14.

[9] John 4:24.

[10] John 14:1.

[11] John 14:9.

touchable, and decidedly vulnerable to sacrifice.

The Spirit is Available. The queen of Babylon heralded before all of the empire regarding Daniel, "There is a man in thy kingdom, in whom is the spirit of the holy gods."[12] Although her pantheism was in error, her advice to the other pagans was not. To this personal ownership of the divine Trinity she rightly defined Daniel as having an "excellent spirit." Of all the false spirits available then and now, Babylon recognized the Person operating inside of Daniel as holy, excellent and uniquely able. This spirit within Daniel was none other than the Creator, the progenitor of Christ, Jesus Himself. That's right! The author of all things, the only Savior of man, and the true judge in the end, was living, presiding and ruling within the lowly slave from Israel. It was He who gave both dream and interpretation, writing on the wall and translation. His Spirit set up kings and replaced them at a whim. Daniel had something far better than a

---

[12] Daniel 5:11.

secret technology, a cosmic smartphone, or an inside scoop. He had the very Spirit of God "excelling" Him to the forefront of all earthly plans. He was speaking to God and for God. The very precise person of God was making all onlookers, and even today's posterity, see what His Almighty Spirit could do in and through a man. That such an amazing power can imbue our own fallen nature with everlasting life is so great a promise! That it can be known and owned seems too wonderful to realize! But it is true. No wonder Daniel survived Babylon. He had an Excellent Spirit. The very spirit of Jesus, the available Holy Spirit, protected him and made him preferred above all the cultists of Babylon. Such a Spirit is available to you. Jesus said of Himself:

"And I will pray the Father, and he shall give you another Comforter, that he may abide with you forever; Even the Spirit of truth; whom the world cannot receive, because it seeth him not, neither knoweth him: but ye know him; for he dwelleth with you, and shall be in you. I will not leave you comfortless; I will come to you." - John 14:16-18.

The Babylonian Alternative. Babylonian religion consists of the original lie from Lucifer in the garden of Eden, "ye shall be as gods."[13] It promises not salvation come from God, but incites a storming of Heaven to become a god oneself. This is where the political heads got the idea to deify themselves. Egyptian pharaohs had the same religion, albeit with differently named source gods. Rome and Greece similarly kept the broken theology, but changed the names of the source gods. This mixing of politics and religion slithered into Christianity, then subtly emerged into modernity, permeating the church into contemporary Babylonian ideals. It crept in unawares through Roman Catholicism, Jewish Kabballah, high level Masonic "mysteries", the sacred geometry of royal gardens and civic city planning, as well as through art, architecture, and music.

Alexander Hislop in his 1916 classic, _The Two Babylons or the Papal Worship Proved to be the Worship of Nimrod and His Wife_, made an irrefutable connection that has lasted

---

13 Genesis 3:5.

nearly one-hundred years, and is even more relevant now:

"In leading proof of the **Babylonian character of the Papal Church** the first point to which I solicit the reader's attention, is the character of MYSTERY which attaches alike to the modern Roman and the ancient Babylonian systems. The gigantic system of moral corruption and idolatry described in this passage under the emblem of a woman with a "GOLDEN CUP IN HER HAND" (Rev 17:4), "making all nations DRUNK with the wine of her fornication" (Rev 17:2; 18:3), is divinely called "MYSTERY, Babylon the Great" (Rev 17:5). That **Paul's "MYSTERY of iniquity," as described in 2 Thessalonians 2:7, has its counterpart in the Church of Rome**, no man of candid mind, who has carefully examined the subject, can easily doubt."[14] [emphasis added]

The divine right of kings was nothing new in the age of revolution but was a European holdout from the Oriental (read Babylonian) construct. The new world had a new opportunity. American forefathers tried to purify both republican government and Biblical faith, offering a

---

[14] Alexander Hislop, *The Two Babylons, or the Papal Worship, Proved to Be the Worship of Nimrod and His Wife*, 2nd ed. (Loizeaux Brothers, Inc., 1959).

freedom from the Babylonian alternative by keeping politics from decreeing a certain religion, and keeping religion from deifying a king. It was the best societal construct ever created, especially as it was relatively King and Catholic free in the United States. Our founders parsed their words well in the first amendment, "Congress shall **make no law respecting an establishment of religion, or prohibiting the free exercise thereof**; or abridging the freedom of speech, or of the press; or the right of the people peaceably to assemble, and to petition the Government for a redress of grievances."[15] This right, extremely well worded and codified, offers something entirely different than the even more modern constitutions of Russia, China, and others. It does not claim a government oversight of religious tolerance, which is still a Babylonian construct, but it proclaims a religious liberty, putting in the hands of the people the ability to keep at bay the Harlot system that had infected Britain, its Anglican state church, and

---

[15] U.S. Constitution, amend. 1, sec. 1.

the rest of Europe. We had, for the first time, from a Christian conception, a Bible nation.

Enter the Dragon. Unfortunately, over time and due to the insidiousness of the Serpent who "deceives the nations,"[16] even America began to deify its founders, idolizing them, spiritualizing them, and creating a presidential cult of personality that invaded the psyche of every patriot. We made them our source gods. Drunk with power, we have adopted the pagan culture and religion of antiquity, covering it with a thin veneer of rhetoric, but practicing a truly Satanic **self-interest**. Finally, we have become, in a new global construct, the purveyors of a Babylonian paganism and the revived Roman electors of a Nimrod-like presidency, which has elevated itself to a near totalitarian threat.

The religious unification under a Roman pontiff and the multi-national union under a global presidency, cemented together in a universal financial order visibly

---

[16] Revelation 18:23.

<u>emerging today is **THIS Babylon.**</u> America is deeply rooted in this unholy arrangement. True Biblical Christian practice is becoming destined for the lion's den, and you must get ready to be a Daniel. Serve Christ with an excellent spirit...for your survival's sake. Only the Spirit of God in a man can endure the coming terror. Following are the specific attributes of this "excellent spirit."[17]

---

[17] See Appendix E: Jesus, About Himself

CHAPTER THREE
Factor One: A Relationship with God

*"[A]nd he (<u>Abraham</u>) <u>was called the friend of God</u>",
James 2:23, (a reference to 2 Chronicles 20:7 and Isaiah
41:8). [H]e was loved by God with an everlasting love,
who showed acts of friendship to him; called him by his
grace, and blessed him with spiritual blessings, and
increased him with the increase of God; favoured him
with near communion with him, honoured him with high
characters, and distinguished him by peculiar marks of
his favour, and reckoned his enemies and friends as his
own; (Genesis 12:8) and Abraham, on the other hand,
loved God, and showed himself friendly to him; trusted
in him, and believed every word of his; readily complied
with his will, and not only yielded a cheerful obedience
to his commands, but enjoined his children after him to
observe them: this was a name which Abraham was well*

known by among the eastern nations;"[1]

-Dr. John Gill, Baptist Pastor and Author, 1690-1771

The Relationship of Friend. Abraham is known as the friend of God. Not just an admirer or simple adherent, Abram, at his friend Jehovah's behest, submits to circumcision, changes his name to Abraham, and then leaves his father's house and homeland to go into an, as yet, unknown new promised home. Friendship with God, it seems, is a relationship that can overcome physical barriers, born identities, parental pitfalls, and even geographic distances. Although Abraham inherited the pagan heritage of his forefathers, the Babylonian spectacles that wrongly imagined God fell off "by faith," giving the patriarch a clear view of the Almighty.

"And Joshua said unto all the people, Thus saith the LORD God of Israel, Your fathers dwelt on the other side of the flood in old time, [even] Terah, the father of

---

[1] John Gill, "Commentary on James 2:23," *The New John Gill Exposition of the Entire Bible,* *http://www.studylight.org/commentaries/geb/view.cgi?bk=58&ch=2, 1999.*

Abraham, and the father of Nachor: and they served other gods." - Joshua 24:2.

Abraham knew intimately of the Luciferian cult of Nimrod and Semiramis. He was versed and surrounded by the astrological tools and star charts of the Chaldeans. The famous ziggurat of Ur was a leftover from the times of Babel, as are all such monoliths of paganism. Abraham grew up in its shadow, knew its priests, and walked to its music, calendar, and culture. Despite all of this religion and a Hammurabi-like god-king (or queen) demanding his worship, Abram sought out the true God of Heaven. His prayers called out for help from a personal God, for a personal connection. He most certainly would have known of the flood of Noah and of the "grace" of God that Noah found. The reading of the stars spoke a different story to Abraham. His conscience was blessed to realize that the lie proceeding from the gardens of Babylon was the same lie emanating from the garden of Eden, "ye shall be as gods."[2]   But Abraham

---

[2] Genesis 3:5.

rejected the lie and bent the knee of his will to become "the Friend of God"[3] instead. Thus he escaped the shadow of Babel, the foreshadow of Babylon, and reveals to us, as he most certainly did to Daniel, the first ingredient of an excellent spirit, the ultimate survival tool for THIS Babylon, a true **relationship with God** Himself.

A Conversation Between Friends. That is what prayer is. Some people make a cold, dead ritual of it. They wash, bow repeatedly, chant rote clichés or even ring a bell as if its voice will carry their petitions. But Abraham was not blowing smoke into the wind; he was having real conversation with a real person. It was meaningful and purposeful conversation like one would have with a real friend. He inquired about the future, shared his inner thoughts, confessed his struggles, and rejoiced about his blessings. God, in turn, gave him direction and reassurance, and made a covenant with

---

[3] James 2:23.

him. Abraham would forever be a part of God's plan for mankind and was promised that his immediate family, one that did not yet exist, would be the gateway family for the whole world to also become friends with God. This relationship Jesus called being saved and born again. This quiet conversation is sometimes just a whisper, but is real nonetheless. Some people do it privately, while others unashamedly pray out loud. All of them seek to become friends with God.

Daniel also had this regular dialogue with the Almighty. Daniel prayed three times a day, "as he did aforetime,"[4] reveals the amount of communication God and Daniel had with one another. It was not ritual, but it was regular. It was not trance-like, but fervent and alive. When the Babylonian henchmen sought to purge the palace of Daniel, they knew they could condemn him in this special relationship only, and so tricked King Darius into making a law criminalizing prayer to anyone but his own image. This is also the practice of modern Babylon

---

[4] Daniel 6:10.

and its political-religious construct. Of course, Daniel continued the prayerful dialogue to which he was accustomed. He was not about to hide his doing so. This is the essence of what has come to be called civil disobedience. When civil powers rule to subvert God, we must simply obey God. We must "obey God rather than men,"[5] Peter repeated almost seven centuries later. What tyranny is threatened by conversation among friends, or what tyrant goes mad when introducing another to one's friend? Only the powers of Babylon show themselves thusly. Ashamedly, the courts, schools, churches, lodges, music, and media of modern America also act markedly alarmed at the simplicity of prayer. Daniel was willing to suffer for his rich and rewarding relationship with God. All residents of Babylon can be equally confident in such a relationship.

A Matter of Trust. Daniel was no masochist. He had no desire to suffer. The realness of his conversations

---

[5] Acts 5:29.

with the Lord, and the absolute trust in God's plans for him, made him confident in a tangible and ultimate deliverance in His hands. If we convene and cultivate a real relationship with Almighty God, the multi-metaled man evil personage of Daniel's vision will try to stomp us out and cut us off.[6] This is a present reality in the global antichristian power structure. We should listen to our friend and trust in His promises. An excellent spirit is made excellent by the glowing proximity of our sure friend, Jesus. When we trust him, fear of man or man's consequences wither away. A lion's den may as well be a playground for kittens. The certainty of our trust is made concrete by the natural communication of our prayers. We memorize and quote His words, sealed forever in the pages of Scripture, as though He was talking out loud to us inside of an arm's length. We trust Him, and amazingly, He trusts us or at least His own Spirit in us. That becomes a wonderful relationship, one that can carry us through THIS Babylon.

---

[6] Daniel 2:31-35.

The Dallas pastor Dr. W.A. Criswell, preached:

"In the tenth chapter, in the eleventh verse, the pre-incarnate theophanic, Christophanic Christ says to him, 'O Daniel, a man greatly beloved' [Daniel 10:11]. And in the nineteenth verse, the same Lord repeats the address again, 'O man greatly beloved, fear not: peace be unto thee, be strong' [Daniel 10:19]. And in the ninth chapter of the Book of Daniel the angel Gabriel, speaking unto him, said, 'For thou art greatly beloved: therefore understand the matter, and consider the vision' [Daniel 9:23]. Three times he is called 'the man greatly beloved.'

There are many people who, studying the Scriptures, will compare Daniel and the apostle John. The apostle John was called 'the beloved disciple' as Daniel is called 'the man greatly beloved.' They lived in such different times and under such different circumstances, but they were so largely alike: their close walk with God, their drawing nigh to the very heart of the Most High, and the giving to them from heaven these apocalyptic visions of the unfolding future. Sometimes John is called 'the prophet Daniel of the apostles and evangelists;' and sometimes Daniel is called 'the beloved apostle John among the prophets.' They were very much in spirit and in heavenly favor alike, the beloved man."[7]

---

[7] W. A. Criswell, "The Beloved Man Daniel," sermon delivered March, 26, 1972.

The relational aspect of this excellent spirit carried Abraham away from the gods of his fathers, had Daniel preferred above princes in Babylon, turned the Apostle John's Roman exile into a sweeping heavenly vision, and thus, can help you survive this Babylon as well.

CHAPTER FOUR
Factor Two: Enthusiasm for a Holy Life

"Success consists of going from failure to failure without loss of enthusiasm." -Winston Churchill

"From the glow of enthusiasm I let the melody escape. I pursue it. Breathless I catch up with it. It flies again, it disappears, it plunges into a chaos of diverse emotions. I catch it again, I seize it, I embrace it with delight... I multiply it by modulations, and at last I triumph in the first theme. There is the whole symphony." -Beethoven

"I studied the lives of great men and famous women, and I found that the men and women who got to the top were those who did the jobs they had in hand, with everything they had of energy and enthusiasm and hard work." -Harry S. Truman

"I know of no single formula for success. But over the years I have observed that some attributes of leadership are universal and are often about finding ways of encouraging people to combine their efforts, their talents, their insights, their <u>enthusiasm</u> and their inspiration to work together." -Queen Elizabeth II

Extraordinary Enthusiasm. Great quotes about enthusiasm as an ingredient to greatness abound in history and literature. Exuberant energy can help any person or cause, even bad people and bad causes. It can speed righteous efforts to the forefront, or it can rapidly pull evil ones to the abyss. It is a fuel, or force multiplier, and a recognizable trait. However, in Daniel's case, the case of surviving in Babylon, it was more than just a discipline. It was a natural by-product of his real relationship with God. The Spirit of Christ permeated his own soul, making his spirit appear "excellent". The pagans could only attempt to put up a front of high energy and counterfeit the results of such "holy" enthusiasm. Daniel's extraordinary enthusiasm was simply a richness of "en theos" or "God in" him.[1] This was the meaning of Isaiah's prophecy "thou shalt call his name Immanuel,"[2] and is quoted by the Apostle Matthew, "Behold, a virgin shall be with child, and shall bring forth a son, and they shall call his name Emmanuel, which being interpreted is, God with us."[3] Such a commodity, pure and authentic, helped Daniel survive Babylon. It is one of the secret ingredients in the victory available to you in the immediate future. When facing great evils, "out-enthusiasm" every wicked spirit, intention, and person. Survive Babylon not with fear, but with enthusiasm for a holy life.

"Ye are of God, little children, and have overcome them: because greater is he that is in you, than he that is in the world." –1 John 4:4.

Enthusiasm's Objects.
Daniel was observably enthusiastic about certain things. He did not cry over his

---

[1] Greek, meaning "divinely inspired, possessed by a god."

[2] Isaiah 7:14.

[3] Matthew 1:23.

lot in life. He did not entreat for wealth, or even freedom. He was internally spirited regarding the things of God. No doubt, he had been taught well. This is an endorsement of every effort men and women make to improve Bible literacy in their respective cultures. Around the world, wherever there is a "Sunday school" effort, there is a better civic product. Daniel had a good portion of Scripture at this point in time. Genesis, the law, the Biblical poetry of Job, David and Asaph, and perhaps even contemporary major or minor prophetic inspirations existed. Equally as important was the "still small voice" of God moving Daniel's conscience to refinement and the "loud clear voice" of angelic messenger bringing him clear vision. In oppressive days of Babylonian despotism, an able hold of the Word of God should be among your chief enthusiasms. Such clarity of Holy Writ made Daniel's risk of rejecting "the king's meat" a clear mandate. He "purposed in his heart . . .that he might not defile himself."[4] Surely, he knew

---

[4] Daniel 1:8.

that wine and swine would have been in collusion with idolatry and debauchery in such pagan environs. Furthermore, his absolute enthusiasm regarding the things that were holy to God became persuasive to others. It moved both the prince of the eunuchs and the appointee, Melzar, to risk their own necks in allowing a new "Hebrew" diet. The diet worked, elevating both Daniel and the other persuaded Babylonians in the esteem of King Nebuchadnezzar. Holy things may become maligned and even illegal, but they are still worthy of your enthusiasm.

Christian Enthusiasm is Persuasive. Such persuasiveness protected Daniel and his countrymen in the early and vulnerable days of Babylon's "re-education camp" for foreign slaves. Daniel's enthusiasm and its persuasiveness is evident elsewhere in the sacred narrative. For instance, when Nebuchadnezzar was vexed by a dream that no one could interpret, he ordered all of the wise men of Babylon killed. They were frauds and pleaded like charlatans for mercy. Arioch, the captain of the King's guard, and no doubt an experienced and bloody warrior, was charged to carry out the killings. He could not disobey a direct order without setting his own head on a platter. But Daniel's enthusiasm in God's ability to decipher dreams and his persuasiveness toward others rescued him from execution by the able soldier. Arioch went to Daniel first, not to kill him, but to try and preserve him. Is it possible that a holy enthusiasm for the Word of God can turn even the highest executioner of Babylonian enforcement into a . . . protector? Could modern global governance and its antichristian enforcement mechanisms be persuaded to allow our interpretation of what they deem un-interpretable? Daniel's excellent spirit preserved him, Arioch, and the other courtesans as well.

Such persuasiveness was taught by Saint Paul:

"Holding fast the faithful word as he hath been taught, that he may be able by sound doctrine both to exhort and to convince the gainsayers." -Titus 1:9.

"In meekness <u>instructing those that oppose themselves</u>; if God peradventure will give them repentance to the acknowledging of the truth;"
-2 Timothy 2:25.

A united theology against God, alive and well today, is a repackaged Nimrodian lie. "Man shall be as god" is the insistence of modern "green", save the earth, climate chaos adherents. They believe that their salvation is in their own hands and all others should be deemed ignorant. "Forget God and elevate the survival of mankind" is the mantra endorsed by Popes, pastors, presidents, and kings. Scriptural truths are deemed hateful and dangerous, just as in Daniel's day. Bible advocates are easy targets, and wicked decrees are increasingly being handed down from courts and congresses. How do you survive THIS Babylon? An excellent spirit is the answer. To what do I apply my trust for help against the tide of excessive rule of tyrannical laws? An unwavering enthusiasm in the promises of Scripture, acted out in brave obedience, persuasively moving every foe, is a vision worthy of trust.

"Not slothful in business; fervent in spirit; serving the Lord;" Romans 12:11.

CHAPTER FIVE
Factor Three: An Attitude "From Above"

"People may hear your words, but they feel your attitude."[1] *- John Maxwell, Pastor, Author*

A Determined Posture. An Excellent Spirit will stand a man upright or posture a woman with true dignity. If this spirit is truly the Spirit of God inside of a man, then it is only God that can prop him up and make him stay resolute, or marble-like. Amidst a palace full of pompous aristocrats, Daniel was compelled to give off

---

[1] John C. Maxwell, BrainyQuote.com, Xplore Inc, 2015, http://www.brainyquote.com/quotes/quotes/j/johncmaxw451128.html, accessed July 30, 2015.

another vibe. It was not only his orations that compelled men, but the determined posture with which they were given. It was not a rant, or a tight-fisted tantrum that allowed his survival in Babylon, but the noble way in which he was scaffolded into place by his master. It was this divine pose of both meekness and kinetic ability that confounded the wise men and silenced the critics over and over for Daniel. Without ever seeming overtly angry, Daniel's attitude represented the potential anger of God. Without flashing a rebellious countenance, Daniel's attitude pushed back against the evil within the powers he was forced to serve. Without any smack of pride, Daniel's attitude was the obvious choice for first president . . .even of Babylon! Paul said it best after he stood in Rome before Caesar:

> *"Notwithstanding the Lord stood with me, and strengthened me; that by me the preaching might be fully known, and that all the Gentiles might hear: and I was delivered out of the mouth of the lion."*
> *-2 Timothy 4:17.*

No such attitude can be successful if only contrived by

human will. Only the bent knees of a surrendered will to Jesus Christ will enable the potent disposition. An attitude that is exalted above all difficult people and circumstances can be powerfully felt in THIS Babylon.

"In painting and sculpture, the <u>posture</u> or action in which a figure or statue is placed; the gesture of a figure or statue; such a disposition of the parts as <u>serves to express</u> the action and <u>sentiments </u>of the person represented." -Webster's Dictionary 1858

This was the foundational understanding of the word "attitude." It was the situation of the subject in artistic renderings that enabled yet unborn generations to interpret the static pieces in a living way. The artist or creator could transmit his meaning and preserve his intent. Take, for instance, the Mona Lisa. It is the most famous painting in the world. The woman's smirk is smug yet playful, aloof yet inviting, pure and yet holds a secret. It is the attitude of intrigue that keeps millions standing in line each year to gaze and wonder at her. There are other telling traits to her meaning. Her clothes, her hands, her direct versus indirect gaze, all impart Da

Vinci's own sense of ambiguity towards her. Is she good or bad? Are we supposed to like her or not? Whatever reason Da Vinci had for this portrayal, his message of wonder was conveyed through the "attitude" of the subject. Such is the masterful design that your Creator has for you amidst THIS Babylon. Your attitude among your detractors is both seen and felt. If yielded properly, it can connect with them and hold their gaze. Your attitude can grab hold of whom God wants attracted, or infuriate those to whom God wants to dispense justice. Your attitude is to be, like Daniel's, the <u>determined posture of God's own intentions.</u> A blatant tool in His hand.

In the Lions' Den. Babylon will give you little choice. Modern, Mystery Babylon has designs of her own on your life. How will you survive? The answer? Like Daniel did, with an excellent spirit. "Christ in you, the hope of glory."[2] A relationship with God still allowed

---

[2] Colossians 1:27.

Daniel to go to the lions' den. A holy enthusiasm was persuasive, but did not stop Babylon's plan for feeding their favorite pets. How does a determined posture, the attitude "from above", deliver from the lions' den? The answer is that it did not. Make no mistake, Daniel DID go to the lions' den, but he did NOT go into the lions' mouths! <u>God painted Daniel into the deathly den, but also painted WITH him an attitude "above" it</u>. Our subject, Daniel, was not a common criminal suffering a common fate. He was the main target of a wicked conspiracy against God. He was convicted of obeying God. That was his posture. Three times a day, windows open, hands outward in worship, and in front of the whole of Babylon, Daniel prayed, "as he did aforetime."[3] There is no greater attitude than the one obtained through prayer. Prayer bows the back, but stiffens the spine. Prayer lowers the head, yet enlightens the mind. Prayer bends the knee, while simultaneously quickening the step. Prayer makes you God's masterpiece. You, like

---

[3] Daniel 6:10.

Daniel, are a public display of the Lord's intent. Is your attitude the reflection of God's hand—a determined posture, or a reflection of self-interest—a faithless cowardice?

A Dire Situation. Daniel's greatest line, his most epic statement, comes from the lions' den. When King Darius cast Daniel to certain death the previous night, he did so as a deceived victim of his own pride. Darius' own entourage hated Daniel's influence and sought to remove him. They targeted the source of his masterful attitude, prayer. The tricked king signed the "Only pray to Lord Darius" legislation. Of course, Babylon today enacts an excessive rule of law and legislates away religious liberty in the name of self-preservation. Darius realized how foolish he had been, but he could not stop the wickedness of Persian law from enacting its brutal code. The King wrung his hands all night and rushed to the death chamber crying out, "Daniel, has your God saved you?" To which Daniel replied, "Ha, ha . . .

revenge is mine. I told you so." Wrong. Daniel's determined posture was one of quiet strength. His attitude, in speech and demeanor, stands as a portrait that all the world should get in line to see and take awe at. Amidst the lions, Daniel speaks, "O King, live forever." It is the Mona Lisa moment of Daniel's incredible story. He did not whine, "Darius, I thought we were friends." There was no pleading, "I promise I will obey you now." The dire situation was the backdrop to the most incredible attitude. In fact, it is usually in such settings that a true excellent spirit shines. Daniel's face must have changed Darius' whole life. "O king, live forever!" It certainly changed the lives of the pagan aides. They were thrown into the lions' mouths. Daniel survived Babylon . . .again.

"Let your light so shine before men, that they may see your good works, and glorify your Father which is in heaven." -Matthew 5:16.

When the tyranny of mystery Babylon forms and conspires against you, find the determined posture of prayer. When you get up from your knees, stand in the grand masterpiece of the moment. Act in the attitude "from above", knowing that it will be, not just your survival, but the very undoing of Babylon itself.

CHAPTER SIX
Factor Four: Priorities from Heaven

Water for Peace
By STANLEY A. WEISS NY Times op ed.
Published: July 13, 2009

LONDON — " *Just days after the death of his father,*
Syrian President Bashar al-Assad was asked to rank the
issues of dispute between Syria and Israel. "Israel ranks
her priorities in the following way: security, land and
water," he said. "But the truth is different. They consider
water to be the most important." He added, "Discussing
this matter now is premature and its turn will come only
after the land issue is discussed."[1]

---

[1] Stanley A Weiss, "Water for Peace," New York Times Editorial, July 13, 2009.

National Priorities. Israel's neighbor and enemy knows her well. Notice President Assad did not mention God as one of Israel's priorities. That is unfortunate. If any place should make Almighty God a priority, it is Israel. But, alas, her interests seem to focus on human interests. She makes a play on religion, but her enemies do not esteem her by it. Syrian plans to defend against or even attack her Jewish neighbor are hardly concerned about her religion. They seek to undermine her priorities: security, land and water. This is not so different from the days of Babylon and King Nebuchadnezzar. Yes, the Jewish identity was clear, but there seemed to be no fear of it then. Israel was just a strategic place between Egypt and Mesopotamia that needed to be aligned with Babylon, by friendship or force. Although the Babylonian culture strived to be all-inclusive, Israel just could not assimilate. God would not allow it. Modern Babylon also decries "all is one" in their political-religious dialogue. The mantra "tolerate" is no suggestion. Exclusive faith, defined by Scripture, is not tolerant, and therefore is not tolerated. This has become a cultural phenomenon. Society is anti-Christian and ready for an Antichrist. While Babylonian rulers were a national prototype, today's leaders are the near perfect product of a satanic priority. That priority is to stop God. Only by doing so can the enemies of God preserve themselves. They have only to alter one of God's promises or plans in the slightest way to claim success. Every time they seem to do it . . . the Lord springs the trap. The enemy's very priorities become the Lord's restraining weapon to destroy them. A nation's priorities reveal its proclivity for true success or for sure destruction.

Joshua gives the real secret to national and personal success. He declares, (the only time the word success appears in the Bible):

> *"This book of the law shall not depart out of thy mouth; but thou shalt meditate therein day and night, that thou mayest observe to do according to all that is written therein: for then thou shalt make thy way prosperous, and then thou shalt have good success."*
> *-Joshua 1:8.*

While the nation of Israel had slipped from right priorities then and now, Daniel had not. His excellent spirit proved it. While Israel declined, Daniel was exalted. Personal priorities will preserve you in THIS Babylon, even though the nations continue to fail to prioritize well.

Personal Priorities. Daniel's priorities have already been mentioned to some extent. A relationship with God, enthusiasm regarding Godly things, and an attitude "from above" are highlighted in his struggle. But another instance highlights a crucial matter on which to focus. The priority can be labeled "self-denial". Babylon was a decadent place by all accounts. Modern Babylon compounds that decadence tenfold. It used to be that decadence was to be found in great metropolitan cities. "London is Babylon" was spoken by its prime minister Benjamin Disraeli in the late 1800s. "Babylon Revisited" is a fiction by F. Scott Fitzgerald about the decadence of Paris at the same time. Who would discount the likeness of Babylon to New York, Tokyo, Moscow, or Barcelona? The sour stench of sin reeks in such places. But the modern technology of the internet and wireless smart phones brings decadence to the individual in an instant. Spiritual harlotry is meant by "Mystery, Babylon," and who can deny its likeness to Rome or even America? Modern pagan spirituality is celebrated on Facebook, YouTube, and Instagram. Our minds and our future generations are sullied by THIS Babylon. Daniel's only option was to practice self-denial. No Babylonian diet. No pagan wine. The greatest example is when Daniel, at the risk of his own life, denies Belshazzar's promise of wealth and degree to decipher the damning "handwriting on the wall." To not step up with a prophet's voice in THIS Babylon is to give in to self-interest. The cost of such self-denial may seem steep, but its true payoff is more important than even your survival.

"Then said Jesus unto his disciples, If any man will come after me, let him deny himself, and take up his cross, and follow me. For whosoever will save his life

shall lose it: and whosoever will lose his life for my sake shall find it. For what is a man profited, if he shall gain the whole world, and lose his own soul? or what shall a man give in exchange for his soul? For the Son of man shall come in the glory of his Father with his angels; and then he shall reward every man according to his works. Verily I say unto you, There be some standing here, which shall not taste of death, till they see the Son of man coming in his kingdom."
-Matthew 16:24-28.

A Proper Balance. Daniel made God's will his priority. He set his own will aside, even the desire to survive, in order that Babylon might hear God's voice. His self-denial made him refuse the king's meat and the king's financial promises, but there were also things he chose not to make his fight. Right priorities mean a right balance. Daniel ultimately allowed the Babylonian identity, the name Belteshazzar, to follow him. He wore the king's robe only after condemnations were meted out. There are lines of demarcation to set in THIS Babylon. There are lines to fight over and even die over. However, there are lines in this pagan reality to NOT make into THE issue. If you are offered the pagan diet

62

of modern entertainment, reject it. If you are identified, even negatively, with God's truth, accept it. When tempted with filthy lucre, ill-gotten riches, say no with vehemence. When provided for with uncanny providence, give thanks. <u>Self-denial is not the refusal of position or pay, but the rejection of self-interest</u>. If Daniel would have made issue with the wrong things, it would have negated the effect he had when dealing with the right things. Priorities and balance go hand in hand and are a part of the excellent spirit of Daniel.

CHAPTER SEVEN
Factor Five: A Disciplined Stewardship

"Opportunity is missed by most people because it is dressed in overalls and <u>looks like work</u>."
-Thomas A. Edison

"The only place success comes before <u>work</u> is in the dictionary." -Vince Lombardi

Stewardship is a Discipline. It requires "the careful and responsible management of something entrusted to one's care." (Merriam Webster online) It carries with it the sense of a trusted slave or trustworthy servant. Daniel was a glorified slave. Having little of his own, he purposed to become a topnotch steward. His faithful handling of affairs for his master, in this case the King of Babylon, led not only to his survival, but also his thriving status as "preferred above princes" by Nebuchadnezzar. Daniel, we are told, was a bright and keen student. He applied himself to study and to work. No doubt, he was up early and to bed late dealing with what would become affairs of state. Under him, the King "knew no damage," as the Biblical account states. (Daniel 6:2). For the persecuted in every form of Babylonian oppression, Daniel's example should be considered. Survive Babylon by serving the truth of God even within pagan confines. Of course, this goes hand in hand with the other elements of an excellent spirit. Not every one of us will find ourselves in Daniel's exalted position, but we can still all apply ourselves to the work of a steward.

"Moreover it is required in stewards, that a man be found faithful." –1 Corinthians 4:2.

Only the spirit of God in you can truly make you excellent and preferred. This perception, even by your enemies, will come about by the hard and disciplined work of a faithful steward. Surviving THIS Babylon depends on it.

> *"Servants, be obedient to them that are your masters according to the flesh, with fear and trembling, in singleness of your heart, as unto Christ; Not with eyeservice, as menpleasers; <u>but as the servants of Christ, doing the will of God from the heart; With good will doing service, as to the Lord, and not to men:</u> Knowing that whatsoever good thing any man doeth, the same shall he receive of the Lord, whether he be bond or free." –Ephesians 6:5-8.*

In the Christian construct found in the book of Ephesians, service of every type: wife to husband, child to parent, or servant to master - even if the authority is nefarious - can still be accomplished if you do it "as unto the Lord." Daniel did this, and thus did more than just survive. Our coming dilemma will challenge us to practice the discipline of enduring "as unto the Lord."

Time is Short. Daniel served for decades, yet always kept one thing in mind. Evil's time is limited. He must have kept telling himself, "Keep working, man. Keep going. God's promises are sure and His enemy's days are numbered!" Prayer time to prayer time was a measure of endurance. Day to day was a sure stepping stone to survival. Sabbath to Sabbath proved of great measure to the poor prophet of Babylon. When years rolled by, the Scriptures prophesied of Babylon's sure end.

> *"And this whole land shall be a desolation, and an astonishment; and these nations shall serve the king of Babylon seventy years. And it shall come to pass, when seventy years are accomplished, that I will punish the king of Babylon, and that nation, saith the LORD, for their iniquity, and the land of the Chaldeans, and will make it perpetual desolations. And I will bring upon that land all my words which I have pronounced against it, even all that is written in this book, which Jeremiah hath prophesied against all the nations. For many nations and great kings shall serve themselves of them also: and I will recompense them according to their deeds, and according to the works of their own hands." –Jeremiah 25:11-14.*

Wow! The astonishing truth that God has determined the growing power and persecuting intention of a Mystery Babylon for us to endure is daunting. The even more astounding realization is that THIS Babylon also has a terrible end. We have a deliverance as sure as Daniel's, and even more glorious. We simply have to bide our time and be good stewards of it.

Talents are Tools. Daniel's talents were stewarded as tools for survival. Dream interpretation, inscription translation, and prophetic heralding may or may not be in your arsenal, but certainly there is some talent-tool for you to steward. Scripture promises a spiritual gift. Today's persecuted can still utilize an excellent spiritual gift from the excellent Spirit of God. This is not a forfeiture to slavery - far from it. It is a God-given grace to endure and overcome it. Consider the overcoming philosophy of yesterday's slaves:

> "Slaves used their talents to deflect some of the daily assaults of bondage. They saw themselves then as strong, valuable people who were unjustly held against their will rather than as the perpetually dependent children or immoral scoundrels described by so many of their owners."[1]

---

[1] "'A Very Valuable Man' Slave Skills, and Talents," accessed July 18, 2015, *http://www.gwu.edu/~folklife/bighouse/panel19.html*.

Daniel had another talent that should not go unnoticed. He was a good steward of men. An excellent spirit made him an able leader, preferred by friend and foe alike. His Hebrew cohorts stood and survived with him in Babylon. They suffered together and they overcame together. In self-denial, Daniel used his talents for others' survival as well as his own. After they prayed with him for God's intervention and succeeded, Daniel as a fine steward lifted them up to positions of influence.

"Then Daniel requested of the king, and he set Shadrach, Meshach, and Abednego, over the affairs of the province of Babylon: but Daniel sat in the gate of the king." –Daniel 2:49.

Survive THIS Babylon by stewarding others to survive it with you.

Treasure on Purpose. Money is one of the great temptations of modern Babylon. Love money and you will fade into Babylon and not survive it. Use money well, and you will rescue yourself and countless others. As stewards of the king in Babylon, Daniel and crew could have gotten filthy rich. Surely, every other prince and president sought to do so. It is a Babylonian virtue. Instead, they helped other captive Jews become trusted arbiters of Mesopotamian wealth. An early form of banking and commerce, the relational commodities of the different provinces were entrusted to the Hebrew slaves as a result of Daniel's excellent spirit and incredible stewardship. Integrity, then, becomes a survival tool in the modern polyglot that is fast swallowing us up.

This stewardship as survival principle is illustrated in the Hitleresque Babylon of WWII:

"Itzhak Stern (January 25, 1901 – 1969) was a man of Jewish faith who worked for German industrialist Oskar Schindler. He was the accountant for Schindler's enamelware company in Kraków and greatly helped run the business. He is credited with typing the list of names known as Schindler's list, a list of Jews who survived the Holocaust because of Oskar Schindler's efforts.

Schindler showed Stern the balance sheet of a company he was thinking of acquiring, an enamelware manufacturer called Rekord Ltd owned by a consortium of Jewish businessmen that had filed for bankruptcy earlier that year. Stern advised him that rather than running the company as a trusteeship under the auspices of the Haupttreuhandstelle Ost (Main Trustee Office for the East), he should buy or lease the business, as that would give him more freedom from the dictates of the Nazis, including the freedom to hire more Jews.

In a later meeting, Stern informed Schindler that he could use Jewish slave labour to staff his factory at a lower price than Polish laborers. Schindler, recognizing the advantage, took Stern up on his suggestion. Stern was said to be able to bring out the strong moral side of Schindler. Stern discovered a way to channel his essentially forced labor for Schindler into a way to help his fellow Jews. As Schindler left Stern to run the factory, he immediately began to give factory jobs to Jews who otherwise would have been deemed "nonessential" and would most likely have been killed. He forged documents to make teachers and intellectuals appear to be experienced machinists and factory workers. Stern's motivation to help his people was abundantly clear."[2]

---

[2] Excerpts from "Itzhak Stern," *Wikipedia*, last modified May 11, 2015, accessed July 18, 2015.

Daniel's stewardship of time, talent and treasure was a key to his survival.

CHAPTER EIGHT
Daniel's Defiance R.E.A.P.S.
Survival and More

"The majority of scribes at a palace or a temple were <u>*working for subsistence rations*</u>*, the same as other artisans, while* <u>*a few attained the status of courtiers*</u> *or high-ranking temple officials and priests and became very wealthy. This more or less even distribution among the different social strata of Babylonian cities,* <u>*without enjoying specific privileges*</u>*, accounts for some of the social solidarity and insights into the lives of ordinary people which mark some genres of cuneiform writing, but it also meant that* <u>*they permeated society*</u> *and perhaps acted as leaven,* <u>*distributing certain traditional values*</u> *such as the respect for learning across a much wider population." "They* <u>*based their view of the world on a wider and deeper base*</u> *than their illiterate contemporaries and were thus in* <u>*a better position to interpret the present and adapt to change.*</u> *Like the*

merchants who travelled beyond the plains of Mesopotamia and who were mediating between city and country, far and near, the scribes and intellectuals mediated between the past and future, low and high, and thus contributed to the richness and vitality of Babylonian culture."[1] *–Gwendolyn Leick.*

That many historians wax eloquent about ancient Mesopotamian culture without so much as a hint of a mention of Daniel, is more a sign of their prejudice against Scripture than a reliance upon pure scholarship. Perhaps they are more Babylonian than not. Nevertheless, Daniel's defiance of the wickedness of Babylon, his reliance on an "excellent spirit" and his very survival reaped a wider fruit than personal historical mention. That his effect is preserved through millennia, and known to have "contributed to the richness and vitality of Babylonian culture", cannot be ignored. Daniel overcame his dilemma with an excellent spirit, was preferred above the personalities of the day, and in

---

[1] Gwendolyn Leick, *The Babylonians: an Introduction (Peoples of the Ancient World)* (London: Routledge, 2002), 94-95.

a sense, conquered the culture. His God within tamed the lions in the den, the false magicians, and even the magistrates. "Babylon" as an institution was tamed and had to be transferred to other environs and ideologies to stay alive. What hope this gives to the faithful, but persecuted, follower of Jesus Christ living in the final form of mystery Babylon!

Christ can conquer the immoral destroyers of sacred marriage, tame the fanatical Islamic lions, navigate through the sinful and self-glorifying media culture of modernity, and foul the attempts of Babylonian purists - whose revival of global, spiritual, and political protocols threaten freedom everywhere.[2]

R.E.A.P.S. You reap what you sow. This is true and from the mouth of God.

> *"They that sow in tears shall reap in joy."*
> *–Psalm 126:5.*

Ignore it, and you will end up shipwrecked. Embrace it,

---

[2] See Appendix D: Secrets of the U.N. Meditation Room

and you will sail with fair winds always. There are probably a multitude of characteristics from Daniel's experiences that could be determined to contribute to his survival and preference in Babylon. Five clear traits have been shared so far in this treatise. An **Excellent Spirit** sows:

1. A **RELATIONSHIP** with God. Daniel devoted himself to loving the very person of God. In return, he became "a man greatly loved", trusted to turn kings and move kingdoms on God's behalf. Can any result be better than reaping favor with the Creator?

2. A holy **ENTHUSIASM** regarding the things of God. Daniel's zeal to obey God, and his happy results, persuaded palace eunuchs and professional soldiers not only to protect him, but to put themselves at risk. What a miraculous reaping!

3. An **ATTITUDE** "above" difficult people and overwhelming circumstances. Daniel could have

78

cursed King Darius, but blessed him instead. "O king, live forever," can only be sown in the lion's den by someone of extraordinary spiritual insight. Daniel reaped safety from the lions' hunger and the king's wrath as he watched his accusers be devoured.

4. The **PRIORITY** of self-denial in order to ensure Godly delight. Putting aside the sure pleasure of the palace buffet, and rejecting the bribes of a tyrant, Daniel delivered, under the sure prospect of death, a damning judgment upon Belshazzar in front of the pride of Babylon. He not only lived, but also reaped reward, and saw Babylon transform into Persia overnight.

5. The faithful discipline of **STEWARDSHIP**. Work not just for your own survival. Daniel stewarded God's people through decades of dangers, sowing his time, talents, and treasures for the sure reaping of prophesied deliverance. He waited, as a fine waiter

does upon his assigned tables, yet as "unto the Lord."

Relationship, Enthusiasm, Attitude, Priority, and Stewardship combine to form the acrostic R.E.A.P.S. Sowing these seeds proves the excellent spirit, and even in modern Babylon REAPS survival and more. Daniel came to the incredible day when he discovered something in the Bible,

"In the first year of his reign I Daniel understood by books the number of the years, whereof the word of the LORD came to Jeremiah the prophet, that he would accomplish seventy years in the desolations of Jerusalem." –Daniel 9:2.

What liberation of heart! An amazing clarity of deliverance! Joy! A smile. Daniel reaped personally and soulfully. Babylon, the revived religion and dictatorship of Nimrod, the golden realization of the serpent's garden religion, oppressive and cruel, mighty and proud, is fallen! Furthermore, he is personally delivered additional rewards from heaven:

"O Lord, hear; O Lord, forgive; O Lord, hearken and do; defer not, for thine own sake, O my God: for thy

city and thy people are called by thy name. And whiles I was speaking, and praying, and confessing my sin and the sin of my people Israel, and presenting my supplication before the LORD my God for the holy mountain of my God; Yea, whiles I was speaking in prayer, even the man Gabriel, whom I had seen in the vision at the beginning, being caused to fly swiftly, touched me about the time of the evening oblation. And he informed me, and talked with me, and said, O Daniel, I am now come forth to give thee skill and understanding. At the beginning of thy supplications the commandment came forth, and I am come to shew thee; for thou art greatly beloved: therefore understand the matter, and consider the vision."
–Daniel 9:19-23.

He is then given what most Biblicists consider the greatest prophecy in the whole of Scripture. It is the vision of 70 weeks of years, which includes not only the precise timing of Christ's first coming, but also of the final seven year tribulation, at the end of which is Christ's second coming. All of this vision was given so that you could continue to survive and ultimately defeat THIS Babylon.

The Greatest Reaping. But that is not all. Daniel reaped not just for himself, his countrymen, and his country, but he reaped the greatest prize of all. Through Daniel, God was glorified in all the earth and for all time as it is recorded in Scripture.

> *"Then king Darius wrote unto all people, nations, and languages, that dwell in all the earth; Peace be multiplied unto you. I make a decree, That in every dominion of my kingdom men tremble and fear before the God of Daniel: for he is the living God, and stedfast for ever, and his kingdom that which shall not be destroyed, and his dominion shall be even unto the end. He delivereth and rescueth, and he worketh signs and wonders in heaven and in earth, who hath delivered Daniel from the power of the lions. So this Daniel prospered in the reign of Darius, and in the reign of Cyrus the Persian." -Daniel 6:25-28.*

Even in the midst of the current apparition of THIS Babylon, which could be the awful and final form prophesied, you can be the instrument through which God receives glory. The very enemies of God may be the ones who decree to the whole world of God's power and might. Sowing is hard work. It can be dirty, hot, back-breaking and tedious. Be sure that a day of reaping will come. Survive THIS Babylon with an excellent spirit. Sow its traits; reap its benefits. Above all, be the beloved agent credited with God receiving what He is due.

PART TWO:
THE EXAMPLE OF
AN EXCELLENT SPIRIT
THROUGH THE AGES

CHAPTER NINE
Daniel's Legacy

"Well, it is unfortunate that Mr. Netanyahu now totally-- distorts realities of today. He even distorts his own-- scripture. If-- if you read the book of Esther, you will see that it was the Iranian king <u>who saved the Jews</u>. If you read-- the-- the Old Testament, you will see that it was an Iranian king <u>who saved the Jews from Babylon</u>. Esther has a town in Iran where-- where our Jewish population, which is the largest in the Middle East-- visit on-- on a regular basis. It is-- it is truly, truly regrettable that bigotry gets to the point of making allegations against an entire nation <u>which has saved Jews three times</u> in its history: Once during that time of--- of a prime minister who was trying to kill the Jews, and the king <u>saved the Jews</u>, again during the time of Cyrus the Great, where <u>he saved the Jews from Babylon</u>, and during the-- Second World War, where Iran saved the Jews. Iran has a bright record of-- tolerance to other

religions. We have a Jewish member of our parliament. It is totally regrettable that somebody plays such a distortion of reality, not only of <u>contemporary reality,</u> but even of <u>Biblical reality,</u> and of the scripture to which-- they claim allegiance."[1]
-Iranian Foreign Minister Mohammed Javad Zarif

"Conversant as he was with both the Bible and history, Truman allowed the two to intermingle on occasion. Moshe Davis recalled a visit the former president made to the Jewish Theological Seminary in New York City accompanied by his former haberdashery partner. During a conversation with Professor Alexander Marx and seminary president Professor Finkelstein, Eddie Jacobson pointed toward Truman and proclaimed, 'This is the man who helped create the State of Israel.' Without so much as a pause, Truman shot back, 'What do you mean, helped create? <u>I am Cyrus, I am Cyrus!</u>' thus evoking the biblical imagery of Cyrus the Great, who made possible the return of the Jews to Jerusalem."[2]
-Michael T. Benson

So the former president of the United States Harry

---

[1] "Full Interview With Iranian Foreign Minister Mohammad Javad Zarif," *NBC News.com,* accessed July 18, 2015, http://www.nbcnews.com/news/world/full-interview-iranian-foreign-minister-mohammad-javad-zarif-n317516.

[2] Michael T. Benson, *Harry S. Truman and the Founding of Israel* (Westport, CT: Praeger, 1997), 189.

Truman claims, as his legacy, to be the protector of the Jews from the Babylonian oppressor, in the form of Nazi Germany. He even channels Cyrus the great. Also, the current Iranian foreign minister Zarif challenges Netanyahu, the Israeli Prime Minister, through an NBC interview that Iran, indeed Cyrus, is the protector of the Jews, implying that they should be trusted today. It is interesting, especially for the naysayers regarding the idea that Mystery Babylon is alive and well today, that players on the world scene do not doubt it at all. They invoke the Prophet Daniel without saying his name. Daniel's excellent spirit was the key survival ingredient. God's spirit in him preserved him and was the moving agent in regard to the royal relationships with the various kings. <u>Daniel's lasting legacy was not the narrative of the lion's den, but the how and why he and others continued to survive</u>. This excellent spirit dynamic was passed on to his countrymen throughout the exile, working to preserve the faithful throughout succeeding generations during the Persian, Greek, and

Roman empires. Your excellent spirit will do more than just help you survive; it will affect others. These timeless truths sown will always reap, and still do. There are many examples.

Shadrach, Meshach, Abednego. There were three Hebrew boys that went into Babylonian servitude along with Daniel. They also suffered from the dangerous people and harsh circumstances that Daniel faced. The R.E.A.P.S. factors were modeled by Daniel and influenced these friends to act in a similar manner. When Daniel's interpretation of the head of gold was given to Nebuchadnezzar, he, no doubt, let it go to his head. He created a colossal idol of gold and demanded it be worshipped by all the world. When the music was played, all knees were to bow. This simply could not be done. The boys, having a relationship with God, enthusiasm against idolatry, an attitude that could face death, priorities that put integrity first, and the firm stewardship ideals of Daniel, stood up straight. Strong and firm, they would not bend. While Daniel is absent from this particular narrative, his shadow is cast over his friends, and they, though thrown into a fiery furnace as punishment for disobeying the king, <u>survived</u>. The Excellent Spirit, Jesus Himself, became visible in the midst of the flames. He delivered the boys before the king's very eyes.

> *"Then Nebuchadnezzar spake, and said, Blessed be the God of Shadrach, Meshach, and Abednego, who hath sent his angel, and delivered his servants that trusted in him, and have changed the king's word, and yielded their bodies, that they might not serve nor worship any god, except their own God. Therefore I make a decree, That every people, nation, and language, which speak any thing amiss against the God of Shadrach, Meshach, and Abednego, shall be cut in pieces, and their houses shall be made a dunghill: because there is no other God that can deliver after this sort. Then the king promoted Shadrach, Meshach, and Abednego, in the province of Babylon." -Daniel 3:28-30.*

Notice the pattern? They had witnessed Daniel's excellent spirit in his reaping the great miracle and benefit of changing the menu in the king's palace. They sowed this same spirit in all of its attributes when challenged with idolatry. Like Daniel, they survived; God was exalted, and they themselves were lifted up. Such a series of events experienced together would have inspired great hope amidst the captives in Babylon. And what if you sow an excellent spirit in the Babylon around you? The idolatry, the sensuous fare of the world's menu, and the wicked decrees coming from the highest seats of authority all combine to form this Babylon. Will not the factors practiced in Daniel's life help you to both survive and thrive in Babylon?

While others invoke Cyrus, and imagine themselves to be saviors against modern Babylonian constructs, the real survival guru is Daniel. He shows us the way to endure, to survive, and to help others make it through. We can glorify God and change the course of empires. We, in some ways, can also be in the shadow of Daniel's legacy. Yes, it is absolutely God that is on the throne working the machinations of geo-politics, but Daniel's legacy shows us how to be the chief instruments of preservation in God's hand.

Ezekiel. Matthew. Mark. These are men who invoke
Daniel amidst their own Babylonian experiences.
Ezekiel was a contemporary of Daniel in the same pagan
world. Of Daniel he records,

> *"Behold, thou art wiser than Daniel; there is no
> secret that they can hide from thee:" –Ezekiel 28:3.*

These words are actually God's words toward the King
of Tyre, a figure of the Antichrist, and a type of Satan
himself. God speaks mockingly toward the devil, but
uses Daniel as the example in his dialogue. It is as
though God jests, "So you think you know everything,
Devil? Are you smarter than Daniel?" God goes on to
promise the king of Tyre's (and thus Satan's) destruction.
Daniel's legacy is very well known to God, and the Lord
would have us reminded of it in our own modern
Babylonian fight against the Devil.

Both Matthew and Mark, in speaking of the end of days,
also invoke Daniel's wisdom. They reference the

Babylonian apparition of a self-proclaimed God-man who will mandate all to worship him.

> *"When ye therefore shall see the abomination of desolation, spoken of by Daniel the prophet, stand in the holy place, (whoso readeth, let him understand:)"* *–Matthew 24:15.*

> *"But when ye shall see the abomination of desolation, spoken of by Daniel the prophet, standing where it ought not, (let him that readeth understand,) then let them that be in Judaea flee to the mountains:" –Mark 13:14.*

Surely Babylon is back, but so is Daniel's legacy! This same excellent spirit sown today will reap similar results seen throughout every tyrannical episode throughout history. The following chapters show this legacy at work in other men and at other times.

CHAPTER TEN
The Persian Expression of Babylon

"The present building of this mausoleum, which is visited by Jewish pilgrims from all over the world, has nothing to speak about from the architectural point of view. Under its simple brick dome there are two graves with some Hebrew inscription up on the plaster work of the wall. Two exquisite wooden tomb-boxes are also to be seen, one of which is of an earlier date and bears an inscription in Hebrew.

The original structure dates to the 7th Century A. H. [13th Century A.D.] and it might have been erected over other and more ancient tombs. The exterior form of this mausoleum, built of brick and stone, resembles Islamic constructions, and the monument consists of an entrance, a vestibule, a sanctuary and a Shah-ni-shin (King's sitting place). Some believe that the mausoleum is the resting-place of Esther, the Achaemenian Queen

and wife of Xerxes (Khashayarshah) and the second tomb belongs to her uncle, Mardocai."[1]
-The Tomb of Esther & Mardecai - Hamadan, Iran

Mordecai in the Shadow. While there is little archeological evidence for Daniel's life, there is abundant proof of Mordecai the doorkeeper. When Babylon gave way to Persia, as Daniel's vision foretold, Daniel fades off the scene. There are several proposed tombs of Daniel, but none is proven to be legitimate. Perhaps the claims of his tomb's presence by rival towns in Iraq are proof enough of his renown. Many ancient clay records remain of the Persian Empire, however, and there are many references to what scholars believe to be the man, Mordecai. If they are correct, then history shows that he was a palace eunuch in high station to the Persian kings who was related to a Persian queen. His name in the record comes across as related to Marduk, but that makes perfect sense as we are given his stylized name

---

[1] "The Tomb of Esther & Mardecai - Hamadan, Iran," *Farsinet.com*, accessed July 18, 2015, http://www.farsinet.com/hamadan/esther.html.

'Mordecai' in Scripture. Furthermore, both Ahasuerus and Esther are found in the record as Artaxerxes and something akin to Ishtar, respectively. Like Daniel, Mordercai and his niece, the queen, were Hebrews given Persian names of the Babylonian gods. Like Daniel, Mordecai was probably a eunuch of high service in the palace. Like Daniel, Mordecai survived the Babylonian ideal, then in Persia, by practicing the humble semblances of an excellent spirit. Like Daniel, Mordecai also had mortal enemies close to the king who wanted his head to roll. The spirit of Babylon continues.

Although undermined by palace intrigue, attacked by tyrannical laws, and plotted to be exterminated, Mordecai and Esther won over the king and the palace servants in order to survive. Sound familiar? Daniel's legacy not only surpassed empires but also practically opened the door for other Jews in the Persian realm to be lifted up into important positions of influence. As Daniel was preferred above presidents and princes, Mordecai also came to be highly esteemed.

"For Mordecai the Jew was next unto king Ahasuerus, and great among the Jews, and accepted of the multitude of his brethren, seeking the wealth of his people, and speaking peace to all his seed."
–Esther 10:3.

Of course, Esther gained the rank of Queen. Not a bad way to survive. The excellent spirit that exalted Daniel and his God also saw Mordecai and Esther through the Persian expression of Babylon. It is the same in every succeeding generation.

Nehemiah in the Shadow. Just as Daniel's exalted status reaped and paved the way for Jewish service in trusted positions, Mordecai's (and Esther's) reaping paved the way for Nehemiah. Nehemiah was a cupbearer for yet another Nimrod-like character. To be trusted to keep the cup of the king was a rare show of disciplined stewardship, to say the least. Anything the king might drink, Nehemiah was to taste first; most everything the king would drink would come from the

98

very King's cup that Nehemiah kept in his possession.
He could have very easily poisoned the king whenever
he wanted. Like Daniel and Mordecai, his excellent spirit
was of incredible use to his survival. At this point in
time, the Jews had begun to return to Israel. However,
news had reached Nehemiah that the city was still in a
state of shameful disrepair. By a humble attitude and
posture, he sought to persuade Artaxerxes to obtain
leave of the king and to travel to repair the city walls.
Great authority, and even great treasure out of the king's
own stores, were given to him for the monumental task.
Again, what a way to survive Babylon! Nehemiah knew
that a mysterious form of Babylon was still at work,
however, and he even attributes the power to that dark
place.

"But in all this time was not I at Jerusalem: for in the
two and thirtieth year of Artaxerxes king of Babylon
came I unto the king, and after certain days obtained
I leave of the king:" –Nehemiah 12:6.

The prayers of Nehemiah were like unto Daniel's own
for the people of Israel. (Neh. 1) "Let the king live

forever,"[2] even rolled off his tongue at the crucial time in his narrative, just like Daniel. There was a proven way to survive Babylon and Nehemiah put that knowledge, and the factors already mentioned, to work. Israel was preserved and God was glorified.

One further point worth mentioning would be that Nehemiah's brother, the man put in charge of Jerusalem, was named Hanani and Hananiah. This is the same name of the compatriot of Daniel who withstood the fiery furnace. Could it be that Nehemiah and his brother were not only schooled together in Daniel's sowing of an excellent spirit, but also that Hananiah was a namesake?

Prophets in the Shadow. Not only was Ezekiel a contemporary of Daniel, but so also were other well-known prophets. Zechariah and Haggai both sat in the shadow of Daniel and prophesied about surviving Babylon. In fact, they also spoke about the spirit of God in the spirit of man, or the excellent spirit so highlighted.

---

[2] Nehemiah 2:3.

Haggai prophesies,

> *"Then spake Haggai the LORD'S messenger in the LORD'S message unto the people, saying, I [am] with you, saith the LORD. And the <u>LORD stirred up the spirit of Zerubbabel</u> the son of Shealtiel, governor of Judah, and <u>the spirit of Joshua the son of Josedech</u>, the high priest, and <u>the spirit of all the remnant of the people;</u> and they came and did work in the house of the LORD of hosts, their God,"* –Haggai 1:13-14.

Zechariah writes of this spirit thusly,

> *"Then he answered and spake unto me, saying, This is the word of the LORD unto Zerubbabel, saying, <u>Not by might, nor by power, but by my spirit, saith the LORD</u> of hosts."* –Zechariah 4:6.

And regarding Babylon he states,

> *"Deliver thyself, O Zion, that dwellest with the daughter of Babylon."* –Zechariah 2:7.

Remember that Babylon, then and now, is a mother of harlots; thus we are to escape her at all costs. We deliver ourselves by having an excellent spirit. Sowing the seeds of an excellent spirit reaps the fruit of deliverance.

CHAPTER ELEVEN
The Greek Expression of Babylon

"The only historical event connecting Alexander the Great with the Jews is his visit to Jerusalem, which is recorded by Josephus in a somewhat fantastic manner. According to "Ant." xi. 8, §§ 4-6, Alexander went to Jerusalem after having taken Gaza. Jaddua, the high priest, had a warning from God received in a dream, in which he saw himself vested in a purple robe, with his miter — that had the golden plate on which the name of God was engraved — on his head. Accordingly he went to meet Alexander at Sapha ("View" [of the Temple]). Followed by the priests, all clothed in fine linen, and by a multitude of citizens, Jaddua awaited the coming of the king. When Alexander saw the high priest, he reverenced God (Lev. R. xiii., end), and saluted Jaddua; while the Jews with one voice greeted Alexander. When Parmenio, the general, gave expression to the army's surprise at Alexander's extraordinary act — that one who

ought to be adored by all as king should adore the high priest of the Jews—Alexander replied: "I did not adore him, but the God who hath honored him with this high-priesthood; for I saw this very person in a dream, in this very habit, when I was at Dios in Macedonia, who, when I was considering with myself how I might obtain dominion of Asia, exhorted me to make no delay, but boldly to pass over the sea, promising that he would conduct my army, and would give me the dominion over the Persians." Alexander then gave the high priest his right hand, and went into the Temple and "offered sacrifice to God according to the high priest's direction," treating the whole priesthood magnificently. "And when the Book of Daniel was shown him [see Dan. vii. 6, viii. 5-8, 20-22, xi. 3-4], wherein Daniel declared that one of the Greeks should destroy the empire of the Persians, he supposed that he was the person intended, and rejoiced thereat. The following day Alexander asked the people what favors he should grant them; and, at the high priest's request, he accorded them the right to live in full enjoyment of the laws of their forefathers. He, furthermore, exempted them from the payment of tribute in the seventh year of release. To the Jews of Babylonia and Media also he granted like privileges; and to the Jews who were willing to enlist in his army he promised the right to live in accordance with their ancestral laws."[1] - Isaac Broydé, Kaufmann Kohler, Israel Lévi

---

[1] "Alexander The Great," *Jewish Encyclopedia.com*, accessed July 18, 2015, http://jewishencyclopedia.com/articles/1120-alexander-the-great.

Daniel Knew First. Daniel's experiences in Babylon forced him to serve God with an excellent spirit. He may not have developed the skills and factors explained had it not been forced upon him. His sufferings and successes sit as an example for surviving future Babylons to come. Through the vision of the multi-metaled man, he warns us of the continuous nature of the pagan construct, and the insidious snake-like slithering of the satanic lie from the garden reaching into modernity. This construct, already defined, is not hard to identify. It is, however, a fight to be had for every generation to recognize its shapeshifting form. Daniel foresaw this great Greek beast. He warns of its unfolding power, and as a result the Jews back in Jerusalem knew of "his" coming. It was, no doubt, the very book of Daniel, and the character of Daniel in Babylon itself, which enamored Alexander the Great. Emperor Alexander already had visions, not unlike Nebuchadnezzar's, that he would be elevated. Like that proud king, he assumed apotheosis, that is, his deification. He mistakenly believed that he was a god crowned from the pantheon of gods themselves. Every Nimrod thinks this of himself. Daniel unveils this mindset for us to see and shows us how to survive in such dangerous times. In fact, he prophesies of multiple such manifestations yet future to him. We should not be surprised that the days in which we live will produce yet another Nimrod, Nebuchadnezzar, Cyrus, or Alexander.

Another Pre-Christian Antichrist. Of course, Alexander conquered the lands of previously designated "metal men," but he also conquered the lands of "pre-metallic men" with Nimrod-like characteristics. From Jerusalem, Alexander conquered Egypt, with its Pharaohs and priests. Alexander became very Babylon-like and, in fact, was an offshoot of the earlier Mesopotamian Babel system. The Egyptian mysteries spread across the planet. They are popular today. Historians like to paint Alexander as tolerant of religious practices in his conquered realms, but the reality is that they were all just different expressions of Babylonian spirituality. Wherever this construct exists, the persecution of real faith exists. Mystery Babylon has always stayed alive. When Christianity began to prevail Mystery Babylon was forced to go underground. Its secret existence has been called the ancient wisdom, gnostic truth, masonic mystery, and the new age movement. John calls it the spirit of antichrist, and even now it is already in the world. It has morphed into every religion and therefore calls itself Sufi Islam, Rosicrucian Catholicism, and Kabbalistic Judaism. We ought not think that Protestants or evangelicals are without this mystic cancer. New age mysticism in the form of yoga, transcendental meditation, and channeling spirits through improper use of tongues, visions, etc., go against Biblical admonitions. Furthermore, an enchantment with Celtic (pagan) music, chorus chants, and the emergent church emphasis on "the self" equates to the sneaking up of THIS Babylon on an undiscerning, unsuspecting Christian church. We have replaced the

"Alexanders" with other church cults of personality on both large and small scales. Daniel would have discerned Babylon in today's church culture and would urge us to serve Christ with an excellent spirit.

Survival Depends Upon It. When the metal man was designated by a divide of the left and the right legs, a simple understanding of eastern and western forms of Babylonianism was to be understood. Both the western pseudo-Christian forms of state religions such as Lutheranism, Anglicanism, Roman Catholicism, and Greek or Russian orthodoxy are but Babylon morphed into phony regalia. Likewise, Eastern forms of Babylonianism also exist in Islam in all of its forms, Sunni, Shia, and Sufi. No wonder they call it ISIS – the Egyptian equivalent of Babylonian ISHTAR. The idea of a United Religion is not new, not original, and not tolerant.[2] It is a laughable satanic ruse which will not go

---

[2] See Appendix A: Mystery, Babylon – The Pope and Presidents do Business Together

away. Each generation is called upon to stand Daniel-like and let its excellent spirit be recognized. The practical skills outlined become necessary for survival. Alexander was indeed moved by Daniel's words over 200 years after they were written. He gave Israel a wide berth of function within his empire. This was not to last forever, but it must have been something to see him give nod to the God of Daniel.

Daniel's metal man empire continues today and is revamping and morphing into the end of days' prophesied tyrannical monster. We have no excuse not to discern it. We have every grace and motivation to be spiritually strong and oppose it. We should exercise the attributes of an excellent spirit so as to strengthen our "Daniel in Babylon" skills. If we do not practice it now, we will be easily overrun in the day of our challenge. There will be a glorious deliverance, a magnificent translation of being is promised. So stand strong in the face of sure persecution and the coming evil. Many survival manuals exist in different forms. For example,

"How to Travel in China on $10 a Day," "How to Live in the Jungle with Nothing but a Knife," and "How to Train Teenagers Without Losing Your Mind." This how-to manual is no different. It is a practical treatise that works.

CHAPTER TWELVE
The Roman Expression of Babylon

"Babylon," from which Peter addresses his first Epistle, is understood by learned annotators, Protestant and Catholic, to refer to Rome - the word Babylon being symbolic of the corruption then prevailing in the city of the Caesars."[1] - James Cardinal Gibbons

Peter's Connection. Even the Apostle Peter declares Rome to be Babylon in his epistle.

"The church that is at Babylon, elected together with you, saluteth you; and so doth Marcus my son."
–1 Peter 5:13.

---

[1] James Cardinal Gibbons, *Faith of Our Fathers*, 111th printing (Illinois: TAN Books Inc., 1980), 87.

History claims that it was at Rome that both Peter and Paul were martyred. The Roman pagan high priest combined power with the military and political chief to become a Caesar. His word became supreme doctrine. They called this man the Pontifus Maximus, meaning "the great bridge builder." The implication is that he was the bridge between heaven and earth. Apparently, men could have salvation through him. Talk about a cult of personality! He was the fulfilment of Daniel's vision of the iron legs and was Nimrodian in character. Having both politics and religion combined into one man, he became esteemed across the empire as an all-powerful god. Most Caesars abused this power, as did all previous Babylonian man-god types. When Constantine supposedly became a Christian around 313 AD, he kept all Babylonian imagery, alive while subtly usurping power over the church. What was often characterized as a protection for the church is actually an injection of mystery Babylon into its doctrine. The infamous Donatist-Arian debates pitted the truth of Jesus' pre-incarnate deity against the error, the original lie of the Garden of Eden, that he "became" divinity during His incarnation. This undercuts the divinity of Jesus, and at the same time allows the Roman idea of man becoming a god to slip into the church. Constantine's baptism at his death was of an Arian confession and from an Arian bishop. Thus the mystery of this Babylon incriminates Rome, no matter how hard they protest.[2]

"The papacy is but the ghost of the Roman Empire, sitting crowned upon the grave thereof."[3]

Peter never claimed to be a pope, but instead declared the Bible to be the ultimate authority. Peter's Bible certainly included Daniel's instruction and example of enduring Babylon. While Peter might not have survived the Roman face of this Babylon, he did speak against such experiential forms of pagan worship. In fact, he minimalized his own eyewitness accounts and glorious

---

[2] See Appendix B: Constantine the Great – Was He a Christian?

[3] Thomas Hobbes, *Leviathan*, ed. J C A. Gaskin, Oxford World's Classics (Oxford: Oxford University Press, 1998), 463.

privileged experiences in order to exalt the written Scriptures as superior.

"For we have not followed cunningly devised fables, when we made known unto you the power and coming of our Lord Jesus Christ, but were eyewitnesses of his majesty. For he received from God the Father honour and glory, when there came such a voice to him from the excellent glory, This is my beloved Son, in whom I am well pleased. And this voice which came from heaven we heard, when we were with him in the holy mount. We have also a more sure word of prophecy; whereunto ye do well that ye take heed, as unto a light that shineth in a dark place, until the day dawn, and the day star arise in your hearts:" – 2 Peter 1:16-19.

Peter also spoke of this excellent spirit we do so adamantly promote. Again, this is not just a positive attitude, but is the Spirit of God in the spirit of man. God alone makes us "preferred above presidents and princes." Such a spirit was promised by Peter to the pilgrims at the feast of Pentecost. Such a spirit is offered to you and future generations.

"Then Peter said unto them, Repent, and be baptized every one of you in the name of Jesus Christ for the

remission of sins, and ye shall receive the gift of the Holy Ghost. For the promise is unto you, and to your children, and to all that are afar off, even as many as the Lord our God shall call." –Acts 2:38-39.

While Peter never went into a lion's den, he did suffer prison. A miraculous and angel-inspired breakout from a Jerusalem prison put the guards in a quandary and unnerved the king enough to make him flee to his own fortress in Caesarea. Peter reaped. Peter survived.

Paul's Excellent Spirit. The apostle Paul also experienced great escapes. His survival was even more dramatic as he was let down from a high wall in a basket to escape Damascus, Syria, and afforded an earthquake to break the prison bars at the city of Philippi in Europe. Do not forget the shipwreck and snakebite survival story. Like Daniel, he had a relationship with God and the indwelling of the Spirit of God:

"And Ananias went his way, and entered into the house; and putting his hands on him said, Brother Saul [that is Paul]*, the Lord, even Jesus, that*

appeared unto thee in the way as thou camest, hath sent me, that thou mightest receive thy sight, and be filled with the Holy Ghost." –Acts 9:17.

He had enthusiasm for God,

"Not slothful in business; fervent in spirit; serving the Lord;" –Romans 12:11.

He had an attitude above people and circumstances,

"Bless them which persecute you: bless, and curse not." –Romans 12:14.

He practiced the right priorities of prayer, pleasing God

and preaching Jesus as the only true God-man,

"I exhort therefore, that, first of all, supplications, prayers, intercessions, [and] giving of thanks, be made for all men; For kings, and for all that are in authority; that we may lead a quiet and peaceable life in all godliness and honesty. For this is good and acceptable in the sight of God our Saviour; Who will have all men to be saved, and to come unto the knowledge of the truth. For there is one God, and one mediator between God and men, the man Christ Jesus; Who gave himself a ransom for all, to be testified in due time." -1 Timothy 2:1-6.

Paul was also a great steward for the Lord, writing

thusly,

"For a bishop must be blameless, as the steward of God; not selfwilled, not soon angry, not given to wine, no striker, not given to filthy lucre; But a lover of hospitality, a lover of good men, sober, just, holy, temperate; Holding fast the faithful word as he hath been taught, that he may be able by sound doctrine both to exhort and to convince the gainsayers."
–Titus 1:7-9.

Paul expected all bishops to have persuasive qualities. May it satisfy the reader that the same attributes practiced by Daniel in his Babylon were manifest by Paul in his.

Roman Babylon Lives. Today the Roman Catholic Church is a mirror of the polytheistic, king-priest, cult of pagan Babylon. The statues of saints are mimicking the cold, dead idolatry of the pantheon of gods that continue to change name and face, but are truly the same devils. Together Rome seeks a United Religion with Mecca and Jerusalem in consort.[4] An unholy fornication is taking place within the United Nations, and it does not bode

---

[4] See Appendix A: Mystery, Babylon

well for true believers. When the Pope and the President cross paths in a pagan festival of Babylonian proportions - watch out. An excellent spirit will be our survival manual, and the sowing of certain traits, our survival tools in such an anti-Christian world.

Dr. Paul Chappell writes:

"Direct physical persecution may not be widespread in America today (although it is higher than ever before in the rest of the world), but there is mounting anger, cynicism, and intolerance even here in the United States toward Christians. And as if that weren't enough, distracted Christians are notorious for their own friendly fire issues that result in spiritual causalities and losses to the cause of Christ, all the more tragic because of their source. So what do you do when you encounter opposition? How do you strengthen your hands for the work when there are others actively working to weaken your hands and cut off your influence or ability? . . . When you are criticized, slandered, or mocked for the cause of Christ, <u>remember that you don't answer to your critic; you answer to the Lord</u>."[5] [emphasis added]

---

[5] Paul Chappell, *Strengthen Your Hands: How Godly Leaders Remain Strong in the Work of the Lord* (Lancaster, CA: Striving Together Publications, 2015), 55-56.

CHAPTER THIRTEEN
Babylon's Modern Expression

"An image will be made of the beast, and all who do not bow down and worship it, and through it the Antichrist as God, will be slain (Revelation 13:15). Such was the practice in the ancient Roman Empire. We are thus being told that the religion of Rome with its emperor worship will be revived as well. Religion must, in fact, not only be involved in Antichrist's new world government, but it must be preeminent, for Satan, who controls both Antichrist and the revived Roman Empire, is 'the god of this world" (2 Corinthians 4:4) and desires its worship with a passion. The woman who rides the beast in chapter 17 undoubtedly represents that world religion, as we shall see."[1] -Dave Hunt

---

[1] Dave Hunt, *A Woman Rides the Beast* (Eugene, OR: Harvest House Publishers, 1994), 42-43.

Babylon has become fashionable as of late. The *Star Trek* saga branched out into a modern expression through the TV series *Babylon 5*. It is interesting that it is called "5", playing on Daniel's vision of the fifth manifestation of the metal man. A sort of revived Rome, yet at the same time a reborn Babylon, is surely what is invoked. The BBC has a TV series entitled *Babylon Hotel*. Vin Diesel stars in the movie *Babylon A.D.* which has occult overtones. Reggae music has a recurrent theme of Babylon in reference to the modern world. The European Union's parliament building is a boldly stylized tower of Babel. The cultic halftime shows and Olympic ceremonies are also brazen in their mystery Babylon showmanship. Why all the attention? Why now? The world is being primed and baited for a new age spirituality aligning with a political vision for "global peace", and believers will be the new enemy.

"The thing that hath been, it is that which shall be; and that which is done is that which shall be done: and there is no new thing under the sun. Is there any thing whereof it may be said, See, this is new? it hath

been already of old time, which was before us."
-Ecclesiastes 1:9-10.

Abraham in Ur. Enoch, the pre-flood prophet, escaped his Babylon by walking with God. Noah escaped his by building an ark. Abraham escaped his by leaving family and homeland. His fathers were pagans in the shadow of Babel.

> *"And Joshua said unto all the people, Thus saith the LORD God of Israel, Your fathers dwelt on the other side of the flood in old time, even Terah, the father of Abraham, and the father of Nachor: and they <u>served other gods</u>." –Joshua 24:2.*

Ur of the Chaldees was an offspring of Nimrod and a predecessor of Babylon. Although Daniel's vision goes forward in time, Moses records the history of this mystery and its ancient evil. The evil that pushed Adam from the garden, and that inspired Cain to murder his own brother, is the same evil that Enoch heralded against.

121

"And Enoch also, the seventh from Adam, prophesied of these, saying, Behold, the Lord cometh with ten thousands of his saints, To execute judgment upon all, and to convince all that are <u>ungodly among them</u> of all their <u>ungodly deeds</u> which they have <u>ungodly committed,</u> and of all their hard speeches which <u>ungodly sinners</u> have spoken against him. These are murmurers, complainers, walking after their own lusts; and their mouth speaketh great swelling words, having men's persons in admiration because of advantage." –Jude 1:14-16.

Abraham was a friend of God and talked with the pre-incarnate Jesus. He both had an excellent spirit with all of its traits and paved the way for us to have it as well.

"That the blessing of Abraham might come on the Gentiles through Jesus Christ; that we might receive the promise of the Spirit through faith."
–Galatians 3:14.

From what Abraham so obediently fled, you may also escape. Finding the R.E.A.P.S. characteristics in his life would be an honorable exercise in Biblical study. The woman that John the revelator saw upon the beast was alive and well when Abraham was alive, 2,400 years before her Roman cloak. Can you see her "emerging" apparition in the modern world?

Joseph in Egypt.

"And the LORD was with Joseph, and he was a prosperous man; and he was in the house of his master the Egyptian. ... But the <u>LORD was with Joseph</u>, and shewed him mercy, and gave him favour in the sight of the keeper of the prison." – Genesis 39:2, 21.

Because an excellent spirit was in Joseph, neither Potiphar nor the jailer could resist the attributes sown before them. They succumbed to the power of God's Spirit within Joseph, helping him to escape evil intentions time and again. The Chaldean mysteries of Ur were not unlike the pagan deities of Pharaoh and the Egyptians. All of this was, of course, prior to Daniel's Babylon. However, the same mysterious woman rode the same beast - religion on top of political power. The faithful were the target from the beginning. Surely,

Daniel must have likened his situation to that of Noah,

Abraham, and Joseph. Pharaoh's question is so very like

Belshazzar's:

> *"And Pharaoh said unto his servants, Can we find such a one as this is, a man in whom the Spirit of God is? And Pharaoh said unto Joseph, Forasmuch as God hath shewed thee all this, there is none so discreet and wise as thou art: Thou shalt be over my house, and according unto thy word shall all my people be ruled: only in the throne will I be greater than thou." –Genesis 41:38-40.*

Joseph came out of a pit and another time out of a

dungeon, but ended up as Zaphenath-paneah, the savior

of the world. This title was given him by Pharaoh. He

rescued his people and glorified his God. Again, it is not

hard to match up the traits Joseph both sows and

R.E.A.P.S. with those of Daniel.

Elijah Under Ahab and Jezebel. Could the

Babylonian construct of a woman riding a beast, or

religious paganism married to political despotism be any

clearer than in the account of Elijah? A state church of

Baal worship was being financed by and enforced by the

king. Elijah prayed against the pre-Babylonian mystery,

so that it, and the land, were struck with a horrible

famine. A showdown, not unlike Daniel's showdown

with the wise men of Babylon, took place upon Mt.

Carmel. Elijah's life was on the line, but just as Daniel

survived the lion's den, so Elijah silenced the pagan's

mouths. Of course, Elijah R.E.A.P.S in the same fashion

as all the aforementioned prophets. Elijah's assistant,

Elisha, knew the secret to the survival techniques of his

master. It is to be found in his spirit. It is an excellent

spirit. It is the spirit of God upon Elijah. Three hundred

years before Daniel's Babylon, Elijah and Elisha

encountered their own mystery paganism.

> *"And it came to pass, when they were gone over, that*
> *Elijah said unto Elisha, Ask what I shall do for thee,*
> *before I be taken away from thee. And Elisha said, I*
> *pray thee, let a double portion of thy spirit be upon*
> *me. ... And when the sons of the prophets which were*
> *to view at Jericho saw him, they said, The spirit of*
> *Elijah doth rest on Elisha. And they came to meet*

him, and bowed themselves to the ground before him." -2 Kings 2:9, 15.

The Roman construct was not a new one. It was a very old one. It was indeed Babylonian. And it goes back further than that. It is as old as the errors of Eden. Likewise, it does not end with Rome. Rome divided into east and west no doubt. The offspring of the eastern and western "Roman" Christian Empire have mixed into the prophesied toes. Partly strong and partly weak, Babylon continues today as modern, technological, enlightened, scientific, humanitarian, and highly cultured. It has embraced us like an octopus, with tentacles of global governance, culture, and politically correct societal "values." It wears the laurels of the U.N. as a Caesar, and embraces the Roman whore, now replacing Jesus with a "green" theology of man as his own savior. Inside of this vise are true believers - persecuted, despised, and redefined as the enemy. Increasingly, we find ourselves the object of the story of Daniel's dilemma, and filling the role of Daniel's defiance. This treatise shows that Daniel's legacy R.E.A.P.S. both backward in history and forward through the ages of empire. Even the American Empire, though glorious, is not immune to Babylon's tantalizing charms.

Now, more than ever, we must exercise an excellent spirit. As the winds of Babylon turn into the modern expression of "hurricane-force" paganized pseudo-Christianity, you will need the proven survival skills of Daniel.

CONCLUSION
What Disparate Enemies
Have in Common

Soldiers Assess Babylon History for Iraq's Future
By Army Sgt. Debralee P. Crankshaw
Special to American Forces Press Service

HILLAH, Iraq, July 22, 2009 – *Multinational Division South's leaders and troops received <u>a tour of Iraq's ancient past</u> here last week <u>in an effort to assess its future</u>.*

The division's commander, Army Maj. Gen. Rick Nash, along with other U.S. military and civilian advisors, received a special guided tour of the <u>famous high-reaching walls</u> and <u>ancient statues of Babylon</u> on July 18 as part of <u>an assessment for preserving and promoting Babylon</u> as a historic and tourism site for Iraq.

"The mission was to <u>educate those on the command staff</u> and some of the primary staff members <u>on the importance of the religious aspects</u> of this country and <u>what there is to offer</u>," Army Command Sgt. Maj. Doug Julin, the division's senior enlisted leader, said. "Even though we are at war, there are some <u>very important things</u> we <u>have to preserve</u> here and <u>help them preserve</u> as well."[1] -From Department of Defense Website [emphasis added]

An American Babylon. There is no denying it. The United States, the melting pot of nations, has conquered and controlled not just Baghdad, but old Babylon. Our troops have occupied it, protected it, and according to the DoD, "preserved" it. It has something to "offer" American military staff. Could we be a part of the prophetic mystery Babylon? Are we akin to the iron-clay mix of toes mentioned by Daniel? Why are our generals "assessing" a dead culture's future, and "promoting Babylon"? To date (presently 2015) these ruins have not

---

[1] Debralee P. Crankshaw, "Soldiers Assess Babylon History for Iraq's Future," *US Department of Defense Website*, accessed July 18, 2015, http://www.defense.gov/news/newsarticle.aspx?id=55213.

been turned into anything remotely close to a tourist attraction, but in the last six years, America has become much more pagan. Is there a spiritual connection?

"Tom DeWeese, President of the American Policy Center, has also been following the rise of occult pagan spirituality. In a work entitled, "Teachers, Preachers and Greens: The Unholy Alliance to Transform America," DeWeese reveals the existence of a well-funded yet covert effort to paganize American society through an assault on schools and churches. He reveals that the Cathedral of St. John the Divine in New York City is the home of the enormously influential Gaia Institute as well as the Temple of Understanding — a politically influential U.N. Non-Governmental Organization. DeWeese describes a pagan "church service" at St. John the Divine:

"As the congregation sit in their church pews in the great Cathedral of St. John, the Divine in New York City, the priest stands at the altar, ready to receive a procession of animals for the annual Feast of Saint Francis blessing. Down the aisle comes a procession of elephants, camels, donkeys, monkeys and birds. These are followed by members of the congregation carrying bowls of compost and worms. Next, to the sounds of music, come acrobats and jugglers. In the pulpit, former Vice President Al Gore delivers a sermon, saying, "God is not separate from the Earth."[2] – Linda Kimball, January 18, 2011

It sounds a whole lot like a Babylonian festival to the conscientious observer.

An American Nimrod. It is a very distasteful thought, that a cult of personality has developed around the U.S. Presidency. It tears at the heart. That the populous no longer needs their President to be a Christian, pro-life, pro-marriage, or even pro-America is telling. Many criticize President Obama for being negligent, ignorant, or inept, but what if he is skillfully doing exactly as he promised? What if he, his advisors, and supporters are simply keeping their promise to "fundamentally change America"? Is it possible that a sitting president would undermine the Constitution with a determination to transition the country into something altogether different? Might America as we know it give way to a

---

[2] Linda Kimball, "Occult Pagan Revival Signals Death of America and the West," RenewAmerica.com, accessed July 18, 2015, http://www.renewamerica.com/columns/kimball/110118.

Babylonian construct with a modern flavor, and a Caesar-like leadership with a zealous self-interest? Furthermore, could a new kind of pope "emerge" in alliance with a new American Nebuchadnezzar to revive the world with a pagan fervor? If you imagine it could be so, then start exercising your excellent spirit. You will need to apply the aforementioned skills in order to get the same harvest that Daniel REAPS. Surviving THIS Babylon is about to become priority number one.

"King Nimrod was a real community organizer. According to various historical accounts, he built the Mesopotamian city of Babylon and other villages around 4000 years ago. He is mentioned briefly in Genesis 10 of the Bible as a mighty hunter and city builder.

President Obama campaigned as a community organizer. Comparing Mr. Obama's suspicious charity work with Nimrod's accomplishments as a city builder obviously slights Nimrod, but there still are many other, more precise similarities.

Initially regarded by his supporters as a great leader, Nimrod became more tyrannical as his power grew. In his Jewish Antiquities book, controversial historian Josephus wrote that Nimrod "gradually changed the government into a tyranny... to bring [his subjects] into a constant dependence on his power."[3] –Randy Fardel, September 27, 2009

An American Daniel. What is called for now is millions of Americans, yea, of Christians around the world, to serve Jesus Christ with an excellent spirit. Sow diligently in the exile through the attributes characterized by Daniel's life. Study all of the other vignettes in all of the other cultures, and see yourself in their survival. "Endure hardness as a good soldier."[4] These principles apply to every culture, race, nationality, age, or economic status. Anyone, anywhere can strive to survive this Babylon. Get started right now.

Every aspect of current anti-Christian culture: homosexuality, Islam, global governance, "green"

---

[3] Randy Fardel, "Nimrod's Tower," *American Thinker Website*, accessed July 18, 2015, http://www.americanthinker.com/2009/09/nimrods_tower.html#ixzz3g49 60pAl.

[4] 2 Timothy 2:3.

morality, communism, and even new "spirituality in science" adherents, have one thing in common, despite their disparate characteristics. They all abhor religious liberty. They are the prophets of Babylon who do not want Daniel to pray, but force everyone else to partake in their wicked appetites. They want the boys to bend to the image of Nebuchadnezzar, and Mordecai to bow to Haman's ill-gotten authority. They are Pharaoh's magicians, but cannot interpret his dreams.

Nebuchadnezzar has a vision, but the Chaldeans can't quite figure it out. They are "clouds without water."[5] Make no mistake - evil is here, but you can survive it! Babylon's final manifestation may be before you, but there is a stone coming! The hope of survival in THIS Babylon is sure.

"Forasmuch as thou sawest that the stone was cut out of the mountain without hands, and that it brake in pieces the iron, the brass, the clay, the silver, and the gold; the great God hath made known to the king what

---

[5] Jude 1:12.

shall come to pass hereafter: and the dream is certain, and the interpretation thereof sure." -Daniel 2:15.

APPENDIX A
Mystery, Babylon –
The Pope and President do
Business Together

The "beast out of the sea" in the book of Revelation is both an international system AND a global personage. This antichrist will, in fact, be the devil's incarnate counter-Christ and a world dictator. His name will be reflected in his number and his "mark" – 666. Absolute loyalty will be demanded. Dissent will be eliminated with impunity. When the seven-sealed book is opened or "unsealed" by the Lord Jesus Christ Himself, the lawless ones power will be unleashed for a season. Seal one will establish global government; seal two, global martial law and war; seal three, global economic control; and seal four, global health "solutions". This worldwide domination by one person will gain acceptance by more than sheer power plays. It will utilize religious fervor and a newfound faith to make the encroaching evil appear to be the ultimate good. The prophet Isaiah warned, "Woe to those who call good evil, and evil good."[1] This "Universal Religion" will be led by a second beast "out of the earth" – the False Prophet - and together with His pseudo-church, comprise the MYSTERY BABYLON of Revelation seventeen. Yes, the woman that rides the first beast, the great whore, the mother of all harlots that commits fornication with the kings of the earth, is about to be revealed. A one-world U.R. (United Religion), likened to the U.N. (United Nations) and subject to it, is already on the scene. This great hypocrisy is no longer a mystery. It is here and it is about to unveil itself!

---

[1] Isaiah 5:20.

In September of 2014, former President of Israel and Nobel Peace Prize winner Shimon Peres, "emerged from a Vatican city audience with Pope Francis," the Jerusalem Post reported, "after proposing a kind of United Nations for religions." He called the "U.N. like organization" the "United Religions" or U.R. "We need an unquestionable moral authority who says out loud, 'No, God does not want this and does not allow it'." (I submit that Biblical Christianity is that voice, but this U.R. will be the Scripture's opponent.) Why is the President of Israel, a Jewish state, conspiring with the Pope, a Roman Catholic head of his own state, requesting him to lead a new United Religion? The False Prophet is thus revealed!

But that was not the beginning of the U.R. In October of 2011, the then Saudi King Abdullah signed a contract to build the "International Center for the Interreligious and Intercultural Dialogue" in Vienna, Austria. This Saudi-financed venture is to be governed by a body of twelve representatives each from Islam, Christianity, Buddhism,

Hinduism, Judaism, and more. "There will be a consulting body of one-hundred representatives from various faiths, as well as academics and members of civil society," according to the Deutsche Well News Agency. They report that Abdullah thought of the idea AFTER visiting then Pope Benedict in 2007. This is an incredible dialogue seeing as the Saudi kingdom, home to Mecca, is one-hundred percent Muslim, ruled by Sharia law, with no other religious building standing, nor any non-Muslim worship allowed in the country. Once again, what is the Saudi King, protector of Mecca, doing getting inspired about religious unity after meeting with the Pope? The new Saudi King Faisal was at the historic meeting and declared, "The thesis is valid that world peace cannot exist without peace between the world's major religions." What thesis? From where does this thesis come? The answer is from the U.N. and the Vatican's Popes.

That same month in 2011, Cardinal Turkson of the Pontifical Council for Justice and Peace helped write and publish the Papal Encyclical entitled, "Toward Reforming the International Financial and Monetary System in the Context of a Global Public Authority." What? According to World Net Daily, Turkson said, "It would seem logical for the reform process to proceed with the United Nations as its reference because of the worldwide scope of the U.N.'s responsibilities, its ability to bring together the nations of the world, and the diversity of its tasks and those of its specialized agencies." Note that Turkson already submits to the "specialized agencies" dedicated to some future religious oversight. Pope Benedict then said, "in the face of the unrelenting growth of global interdependence, there is a strongly felt need, even in the midst of a global recession, for a reform of the United Nations Organization, and likewise of economic institutions and international finance, so that the concept of the family of nations can ACQUIRE REAL TEETH." These proposed

teeth are the very iron teeth of Daniel's vision in chapter
7:7. There we see the end times beast "dreadful and
terrible, and strong exceedingly; and it had *great iron*
teeth: it devoured and brake in pieces, and stamped the
residue with the feet of it: and it was diverse from all the
beasts that were before it; and it had ten horns."

A United Religion Initiative already existed in 2007 when
Pope Francis, then a Cardinal in Argentina, was pictured
at a gathering in Latin America on the tenth anniversary
of its charter. Archbishop John Quinn was at the
formation of said project in San Francisco at the Presidio
in June 1995. Also in attendance? Among a host of global
personalities, U.N. General Secretary Boutros-Ghali and
Archbishop Renato Martino, the Vatican nuncio to the
U.N. It goes back even farther than that. In fact,
Religions for Peace, a U.N. NGO headquartered at the
U.N. in New York, was co-founded in 1960 by Cardinal
John Wright, for an important "unofficial" Vatican
channel for interreligious activities, according to
Cardinal Francis Arinze, also a former head of the

Pontifical Council for Interreligious Dialogue. Its first international president was Archbishop Angelo Fernandes of New Delhi. Its first interfaith conference at the Vatican had Pope John Paul as its opening speaker! The evidence for the support of a one-world religion with the Pope as its head goes back as far as you want to investigate it. But the difference now is that Pope Frances has the leaders of both Jerusalem and Mecca in willing accord.

On April 28, 2015, this year, the U.N. chief Ban Ki-Moon, at a Vatican conference, hailed the Pope for his coming June encyclical that "will convey to the world that protecting our environment is an urgent moral imperative and a sacred duty for all people of faith and people of conscience." The Pope's New Religion will involve the "sacred duty" of earth worship, and deifying the coming "savior"-beast who will rule it under the doctrine of "sustainability" from the bible of the U.N. charter. Ban Ki-Moon has also welcomed the pending visit to U.N. headquarters by Pope Francis, scheduled for

September 25th. The Pope will address the U.N. General

Assembly, and according to Ki-Moon's hopes, "will

inspire the international community to redouble its

efforts to achieve human dignity for all through ensuring

greater social justice, tolerance and understanding

among all of the world's peoples." Francis will speak to

a joint session of Congress in Washington D.C. (a first for

any Pope ever) on September 24th. Will the U.R. officially

manifest in the United States this fall? Will global

government and global religion unite (the "fornication"

in Revelation 17) in front of America and the World to

usher in a supposed era of false peace? Could this

happen in D.C. on the 24th or in N.Y.C. on the 25th, right

between the blowing of the shofar trumpet signaling the

Feast of Trumpets (a picture of the rapture of the saints)

on September 13th, and the fourth blood moon (an

expected promise regarding the temple mount in

Jerusalem) on September 28th? It seems so, dear readers.

A real sign of the times is before our very eyes.

Another clue as to the importance of this Fall's dates is that on May 13, 2014, Secretary of State John Kerry and French Foreign Minister Laurent Fabius, at the State Department, announced that we have "500 days to avoid Climate Chaos." Amazingly, 500 days from that day is September 24, 2015. Again, this is the date of Francis' speech to Congress, the day before his speech to the World in NYC. This is, no doubt, "the mother of all" spiritual harlotry, and is certainly worthy of our attention. Evil intentions and cryptic mysteries are about to manifest literally. This personage, made real, will be the enemy of God and every Christian. Believe not her lies; reject her liars! Revelation chapter 18 tells of the absolute downfall and destruction of this configuration of evil in the last days, and tells true believers to rejoice in the same destruction![2]

"Rejoice over her, thou heaven, and ye holy apostles and prophets; for God hath avenged you on her."
-Revelation 18:20.

---

[2] Reprinted from the Spring/Summer 2015 issue of the *Immanuel Alive* newspaper published in Corunna, MI.

APPENDIX B
Constantine the Great – Was He a Christian?

Christianity and Rome were at odds since the days of Christ's birth. Roman personalities helped condemn and crucify Jesus, Paul, and Peter. However, the faith spread in the heart of people and overran the empire itself. The Emperor Constantine lived and reigned during this crossroads of history.

Constantine the Great must be understood in the context of the Roman Empire. Diocletian preceded Constantine with Christian persecutions and a government administered by four heads. Called a tetrarchy, it had two Caesar Augustus' and two sub-Caesars.

Born on February 27, 272 AD in Serbia, Constantine's full name was Flavius Valerius Aurelius Constantinus Augustus. He was born to a common mother named Helena and a father, future Tetrarch Constantinius. He was educated in literature, philosophy, and Greek in Diocletian court and was exposed to both pagan and Christian personalities. He campaigned widely for Rome in Asia, on the Danube river, against the Persians in Syria, and in Mesopotamia.

Constantine was voted Caesar upon the death of his Father in 306 AD. He fought the Picts on Hadrian's Wall, and built up the Roman town of Trier, Germany. His ascension to power happened at York, England, then called Eburacum. He had jurisdiction over Brittania, Gaul, Spain, and parts of Germany.

The popular Caesar began to consolidate his power by defeating Caesar Maxentius, who held sway over Italy and North Africa but was greatly disliked. He had a vision, and saw a sign in the sky. It was the Greek letters Chi (X) over writ by a Rho (P), which are the first two letters in the name Christ. A voice was heard saying, "With this sign you conquer". All soldiers were made to put that sign on their shields, as opposed to old pagan icons, before battling Maxentius' troops. The battle was won despite being outmanned. Maxentius died at the Battle of the Malvian Bridge outside of Rome. The West was won, but the East had yet to be conquered. Another Caesar, Licinius, was defeated in a series of battles and intrigues to finally win the East, which included Greece, Turkey, the Levant, and Egypt. The Edict of Milan was issued in 313 AD, ensuring toleration for all religions including Christianity.

In 325 AD, a Christian council of bishops was held at Nicaea to debate the nature of Jesus' divinity. Arius declared Jesus a made being, while the overwhelming majority decreed the Trinitarian doctrine of Christ's status as coequal with the Father. Constantine commissioned Eusebius, Bishop of Rome, to make 50 copies of the Scriptures for use in the churches.

Constantine united the Empire and reinstituted dynastic

succession by passing the Emperorship to his sons. He built three great churches: old Saint Peter's Basilica in Rome, The Church of the Holy Apostles in Constantinople (which became the new capital of the empire with Rome being the western counterpart) and the Church of the Holy Sepulchre in Jerusalem.

Constantine the Great, also called the First and Saint Constantine, died on May 22, 337 AD in Turkey. Before he died, he was baptized by request by an Arian bishop, practically endorsing the errant doctrines and recanting the Nicene creed. Rome had twenty-three succeeding emperors until 476 AD, when the Western empire was overrun. However, the Eastern (or Byzantine) Empire continued for over a thousand years with Constantinople (or modern day Istanbul, Turkey) being the capital, until 1453 AD when the Ottoman and Muslim empire overran it. The final and 97th Byzantine emperor was named Constantine the 13th.

Constantine was one of the more successful and important emperors of the Roman empire and ensured its continuance by building Constantinople. His uniqueness lay in his supposed conversion to Christianity and governmental tolerance of that faith. However, his mixing of State governance with religious enforcement created the apostate form of Christianity called the Roman Catholic church today. He did side against the Donatists, earlier predecessors of Anabaptist tradition, and continued to identify with old Roman pagan deities and tradition; therefore, I do not believe he was a born again believer, but a culturally identified and nominal Christian only.[1]

---

[1] Written in conjunction with the Immanuel Baptist School History Fair, March 2015.

APPENDIX C
Undermining the Nation State

The benefits of modern life such as the world wide web, jet travel, and free trade have definitely made the world seem like a smaller place. The fostering of economic interdependency is known as 'globalization', and, by itself, poses no threat to the Biblical model of geopolitics known as the 'nation-state' model; however, along with this "flatter world" phenomenon has come the renewal of another model. It is, historically, the darker, more deceptive worldview of a one world empire now popularized as 'globalism'. Globalization is a recognizing of effective national principles and practices benefiting any society, then kneading these same principles into prosperity and peace. The United States, Japan, and Germany have become leaders in globalization and reaped it's benefits. They have done so without compromising national sovereignty. Globalism, however, is the antithesis of such proven methodology, and seeks to remove or rewrite not only national boundaries, but the successful national values that brace any country's vibrancy. Utopian one world dream-chasers camouflage their intentions by confusing the distinctions between globalization and globalism, and by creating international platforms for heralding a new world order. There can be no mistaking that the philosophical framework of the modern United Nations and the European Union makes them the chief heralds for globalism seeking to undermine the nation state.

Failure of the Nations. When nations forget God, they also stray from the handbook of societal life, the Bible. The globalization vs. globalism conflict is an ancient one that started in the book of Genesis. God decrees that man should have dominion over his creation as his servant. The serpent likewise supposes that man should be dominant over creation as God's equal. These words are more than semantics, and have had far reaching results. Man has wrongly chosen the latter path. This insidious rebellion has continued and is reflected in both personal and national failures. Some countries have rightly recognized "God given liberties", while others have "mandated state allowed activities". These are age old differences reflected in such contrasts as capitalism vs. communism, and democracy vs. dictatorship. The Satanic strategies of globalism are only attractive where national policies have failed and become repressive. Bible advocates have flourished in the United States and have thusly been able to counter or offset American failures, but what happens when the Bible advocates are marginalized?

Super Power Polarization. These two contrasting national approaches have historically squared off in a regional and now global polarization of competing ideas. David and Goliath like showdowns are seen in times past, with Hebrew and Philistine philosophies squaring off in conflict after conflict. This cycle of war in culture and in arms continues to polarize societies, continents and worldviews. Today there are many who view the world as a divine creation, under God's control and destiny, divided into nations who either do or do not reflect Biblical views and values. There are equally as many, and perhaps a great many more, perspectives who see the globe as a universal body, to be singularly governed by man, for man; who see the Judeo Christian ethic (The Bible) as the chief obstacle to planetary salvation. Sometimes competing globalist views unite around this one common thread; "Biblical thought is poison."

Global Economics. It is this distaste and distrust for

the Bible foundation of good society that formulates the hypothesis and proceeding actions of globalists. A global economics is about more than money. It is not the same as, or as simple as, just the globalization of markets. It is the re-defining of the foundational elements of the command and control of people. It is the attempt to eradicate Scriptural influence and replace it with humanistic values like, "we know what is best for mankind", and "our ecological views will bring forth salvation." The United Nations has been a breeding ground for such dogmas, and have as their supposed authority, not only international laws and agencies, but a host of NGO's that attempt to coalesce their raw philosophy with what touches the hearts of ordinary people, thus by passing the nation state proper and perverting the masses directly. Only Biblical concepts and their advocates can postulate and effect good government with the results being successful nation states; and only Scriptural nation states can fight off the serpentine squeeze into a Babel like order that raises its head again in Revelation's pages.[1]

"And the LORD God said unto the woman, what is this that thou hast done? And the woman said, The serpent beguiled me, and I did eat." - *Genesis 3:13*

"How art thou fallen from heaven, O Lucifer, son of the morning! How art thou cut down to the ground which didst weaken the nations!" - *Isaiah 14:12.*

"But I fear, lest by any means, as the serpent beguiled Eve through his subtilty, so your minds should be corrupted from the simplicity that is in Christ." - *2 Corinthians 11:3.*

"And the great dragon was cast out, that old serpent, called the Devil, and Satan, which deceiveth the whole world: he was cast out into the earth, and his angels were cast out with him." - *Revelation 12:9.*

---

[1] Reprinted from The Bible Nation Society website, http://www.biblenation.org/2009/03/undermining-the-nation-state.

APPENDIX D
Secrets of the U.N. Meditation Room

If the U.N. building is a temple of global identity, then the Meditation Room is a 'Holy of Holies' to the adherents of it's esoteric, pantheistic neo-pagan spirituality. The room was designed by the then Secretary General of the U.N. Dag Hammerskjold, and opened in 1957 as a "meeting of light, of the sky, and the earth . . .", "dedicated to silence, . . .and stillness . . ." , "where the doors may be open to the infinite lands of thought and prayer." (Hammerskjold in his own words).

The abstract mural seen here is a series of inter-related

geometric patterns meant to create a contemplative 'unity of god, earth, and time' sensation. The underlying astro-physiological meaning is the subject of much debate. Could the painting contain a cosmic calendar or message delineating the "Age of Aquarius"? The walls truncate like a pyramid to focus on the cultic shapes, and a simple change in lighting brings different elements to the forefront sparking even more 'meditative ecstasy'.

"But the stone in the middle of the room has more to tell us. We may see it as an altar, empty not because there is no God, not because it is an altar to an unknown god, but because it is dedicated to the God whom men worship under many names and in many forms." (Hammerskjold in his own words). Obviously, this is a Satanic delusion because we know that God's name is the Jehovah of Israel, and his form is that of Jesus of Nazareth. He, the God of the Bible, said,

> *"Thou shalt not make unto thee any graven image, or any likeness of any thing that is in heaven above, or that is in the earth beneath, or that is in the water under the earth." –Exodus 20:4.*

This six and a half ton rectangular block of iron ore polished at the top and lit from above was a present from the king of Sweden. It is meant to be the final resting space of the "Ark of Hope." This mockery of the Biblical Ark of the Covenant, is covered on each side by representations of earth, wind, fire and water. It contains a pseudo 'Ten Commandments' made up of a sixteen point value system expounding the virtues of a 'creation (vs. creator) centered theology'. This theology is the GAIA, or mother earth gospel now sweeping the globe in various forms of 'green' morality and environmental practices.

This brazen show of "New Age" religion adopted by the international community as a hope for peaceful co-existence on the earth, is really nothing new at all, but simply promises that same old lie "ye shall be as gods." Hammerskjold boasts, "There is an ancient saying that the sense of a vessel is not in its shell but in the void. So it is with this room. It is for those who come here to fill the void with what they find in their center of stillness."[1]

---

[1] Reprinted from The Bible Nation Society website, http://www.biblenation.org/2009/03/secrets-of-the-un-meditation-room.

APPENDIX E
Jesus, About Himself

The Old Testament has many prophecies of the future Messiah. This savior of mankind was to be the God-man born in Bethlehem, from a virgin womb, and of the lineage of King David. His name, character, personality and manner of life were all foretold by the Patriarchs and Prophets. A simple study of these prophecies and fulfillments has led millions to declare that Jesus is that chosen one.

"Tell ye, and bring them near; yea, let them take counsel together: who hath declared this from ancient time? who hath told it from that time? have

163

not I the LORD? and there is no God else beside me; a just God and a Saviour; there is none beside me." -Isaiah 45:21.

Likewise, the New Testament records and reports that Jesus was indeed this Messiah. The gospels are overlapping histories, the epistles are legal, theological and practical defenses of his divine identity, and the Revelation "reveals" Him as the Son of God, coming again as a universal King of Kings. He came the first time as a lamb, He comes the next time as a lion.

"And one of the elders saith unto me, Weep not: behold, the Lion of the tribe of Juda, the Root of David, hath prevailed to open the book, and to loose the seven seals thereof." -Revelation 5:5.

But the most compelling of the Scriptures' evidences are the words of Jesus about . . . himself!

Here are some of Jesus' words about himself from the Gospel of John:

1. "For God so loved the world, that he gave his only begotten Son, that whosoever believeth in him should not perish, but have everlasting life. For God sent not his Son into the world to condemn the world; but that the world through him might be saved. He that believeth on him is not condemned: but he that believeth not is condemned already, because he hath not believed in the name of the only begotten Son of God."
-John 3:16-18.

Jesus explains to you His origin as "begotten" from God, His purpose to "save" your soul from perishing, and His method as "believing" in His name. Do you believe that the name of Jesus, "Yeshua" in the Hebrew language, is the name of the chosen Messiah?

2. "God is a Spirit: and they that worship him must worship him in spirit and in truth. The woman saith unto him, I know that Messias cometh, which is called Christ: when he is come, he will tell us all things. Jesus saith unto her, I that speak unto thee am he." -John 4:24-26.

Jesus reveals that He is the Christ, the promised Messiah that would come. Are His words speaking to you in the same way He spoke to the woman at the well?

3. *"Verily, verily, I say unto you, He that heareth my word, and believeth on him that sent me, hath everlasting life, and shall not come into condemnation; but is passed from death unto life. Verily, verily, I say unto you, The hour is coming, and now is, when the dead shall hear the voice of the Son of God: and they that hear shall live. For as the Father hath life in himself; so hath he given to the Son to have life in himself;"*
-John 5:24-26.

Jesus claims His word can be "heard" or understood, and that believing on His divine identity and mission gives "everlasting life", defeating "death". In addition, He claims to have the same "life" giving authority and ability in "Himself" that God has. Can you hear His voice? Do you believe He was sent to save you? Do you know that He has the power to give you life beyond your death?

4. *"And Jesus said unto them, I am the bread of life: he that cometh to me shall never hunger; and he that*

believeth on me shall never thirst. But I said unto you, That ye also have seen me, and believe not. All that the Father giveth me shall come to me; and him that cometh to me I will in no wise cast out. For I came down from heaven, not to do mine own will, but the will of him that sent me. And this is the Father's will which hath sent me, that of all which he hath given me I should lose nothing, but should raise it up again at the last day. And this is the will of him that sent me, that every one which seeth the Son, and believeth on him, may have everlasting life: and I will raise him up at the last day."
-John 6:35-40.

Jesus identifies Himself as the "bread" of life. Partaking of Him by faith He claims will forever satisfy hunger and thirst. He proclaims that He is sent by God, doing God's will, and will "raise" believing people to "everlasting life". God has souls to save. It is a surety. Jesus has and will save every last one that "believeth on him". Will you eat this bread and receive this life?

5. "Then spake Jesus again unto them, saying, I am the light of the world: he that followeth me shall not walk in darkness, but shall have the light of life."
-John 8:12.

Jesus identifies Himself as the "light" of the world. He promises those that "follow" will not experience spiritual "darkness", but own a life of spiritual "light". Many claim to be bright, and offer life, but Jesus' promise is authoritative, unique, exclusive. If you want out of darkness and into light then follow Jesus.

6. *"Jesus heard that they had cast him out; and when he had found him, he said unto him, Dost thou believe on the Son of God? He answered and said, Who is he, Lord, that I might believe on him? And Jesus said unto him, Thou hast both seen him, and it is he that talketh with thee. And he said, Lord, I believe. And he worshipped him." -John 9:35-38.*

Jesus did what no man of God or angel would allow. He received worship as God. He expressed that He was visible and talking in the flesh, and at the same time . . . God. He was both God and Man without sin; the perfect acceptable Lamb to be offered for you. Believe in Him as the Son of God. Worship Him as your Savior.

7. "Then said Jesus unto them again, Verily, verily, I say unto you, I am the door of the sheep. All that ever came before me are thieves and robbers: but the sheep did not hear them. I am the door: by me if any man enter in, he shall be saved, and shall go in and out, and find pasture. The thief cometh not, but for to steal, and to kill, and to destroy: I am come that they might have life, and that they might have [it] more abundantly. I am the good shepherd: the good shepherd giveth his life for the sheep." -John 10:7-11.

Jesus explains Himself to be a good shepherd, one that sits in the sheepfold door as the "door" itself. No enemy and no sheep can enter but through Him. He is willing to give His life for the sheep. Anyone who offers sheep anything less is a "thief and robber". When Jesus says of Himself, He is the door, sheep have "life more abundantly". Heaven's only door is Jesus. The only "shepherd" that can take you through death unto Heaven is Him. Can you hear His words?

8. "My sheep hear my voice, and I know them, and they follow me: And I give unto them eternal life; and they shall never perish, neither shall any man pluck them out of my hand. My Father, which gave them me,

*is greater than all; and no man is able to pluck them
out of my Father's hand. I and my Father are one.
Then the Jews took up stones again to stone him."
-John 10:27-31.*

Jesus has a flock. They hear Him, and follow Him. They

never perish and can't be defeated. The most incredible

part is that He claimed to be equal with God. "I and my

Father are one." The religious Jews knew what He was

claiming. They knew he was declaring to be the Messiah.

Because they were not His flock and did not hear, they

tried to stone Him for blasphemy. Any man that makes

such claims must be judged . . . Messiah, deceiver, or mad

man? Put down your stone, hear His voice, and follow

Him.

9. *"But I know, that even now, whatsoever thou wilt
ask of God, God will give it thee. Jesus saith unto her,
Thy brother shall rise again. Martha saith unto him,
I know that he shall rise again in the resurrection at
the last day. Jesus said unto her, I am the resurrection,
and the life: he that believeth in me, though he were
dead, yet shall he live: And whosoever liveth and
believeth in me shall never die. Believest thou this?*

She saith unto him, Yea, Lord: I believe that thou art the Christ, the Son of God, which should come into the world." -John 11:22-27.

Jesus received Martha's declaration of Himself as the Messiah. She believed His declaration of resurrection power, that is the ability to give life to the dead. In fact, He said if we "believeth in Him" we should never really die. He claimed not just to have power, but to be the power itself. You go to the doctor to preserve your body; will you go to Jesus to forever preserve your body and soul?

10. *"Let not your heart be troubled: ye believe in God, believe also in me. In my Father's house are many mansions: if it were not so, I would have told you. I go to prepare a place for you. And if I go and prepare a place for you, I will come again, and receive you unto myself; that where I am, there ye may be also. And whither I go ye know, and the way ye know. Thomas saith unto him, Lord, we know not whither thou goest; and how can we know the way? Jesus saith unto him, I am the way, the truth, and the life: no man cometh unto the Father, but by me. If ye had known me, ye should have known my Father also: and*

from henceforth ye know him, and have seen him." -
John 14:1-7.

Jesus wants you to believe in Him the way most men
believe in God. He claims not to be one of many ways to
salvation, but "the way", the only way. He does not
claim to be among teachers of truth, but "the truth" itself,
the exclusive truth. He tells not of a better life, but
identifies Himself as the single "embodiment" of life.
"No man", religious or otherwise, can go to Heaven, that
is "come to the Father", except through "Him". What an
incredibly exclusive proposition! It is true or it is not?
What is your response to such a claim? What if it is true?

These incredible words of Jesus about Himself are clearly
loving declarations teaching you who He really is. He is
the promised Messiah! He is all that the New Testament
declares Him to be! He truly declares Himself the Son of
God, one with the Father, having the power to save, and
give eternal life. Furthermore, He receives worship

along with declarations of His identity as savior, and charges you to believe in Him, His name and His saving power.

Many say, "Jesus never claimed to be what Christians today say He is." Nothing could be further from the truth. He not only claimed divinity, but declared Himself to be exclusive and the absolute single way to salvation and Heaven. Jesus was a great moral teacher and enlightener, but He was so much more than that . . . His teachings and enlightenment were about Himself!

He would have you to be convinced of His Lordship today!

"Believe on the Lord Jesus Christ and thou shalt be saved and thy house!" - Acts 16:31.

Repent of your own sins and sinfulness. Let go of the religion of doing or earning your own way. If you could do it yourself then Christ's words are meaningless, and

His cross and death are too. No church, priest, preacher or denomination can save through membership or righteous acts. Only the sacrificial blood, death, burial, and resurrection of Jesus Christ will save your soul and seal your eternity in Heaven!

Bend the knees of your will in humility. Raise the hands of your heart in surrender. Pray to Him, "Lord have mercy on my soul and save me from my sin, myself and my silly attempts at cold, dead religion."

> *"The Lord is not slack concerning his promise, as some men count slackness; but is longsuffering to us-ward, not willing that any should perish, but that all should come to repentance." -2 Peter 3:9.*

Will you believe in Jesus' own words about Himself?

-Dr. Douglas Levesque

ABOUT THE AUTHOR

Dr. Douglas Levesque is the founder of a 21st century think tank called The Bible Nation Society. He is also the Pastor Emeritus of Immanuel Baptist Church in Michigan where he planted and led that body for over 20 years. He has been married to his wife, Amy, for 24 years. They have five sons and all enjoy backpacking, basketball, and reading.

Dr. Levesque's articles may be found on the website www.BibleNation.org.